Just As I Am

AIMÉE REBECCA

Editor: Claire Strombeck
Cover Photography: Laura Carys

This book is dedicated to anyone who has ever been made to feel like they're not good enough. Use this book as a reminder that you are enough just as you are.

Foreword

With the benefit of hindsight (and a lot of therapy), it's fair to say that my past dating record is, quite frankly, disastrous. For years, I tumbled from one dysfunctional relationship to the next. Every now and then I'd pause briefly to swear off men for life, but before long I'd hurl myself back into the chaos and find myself swept off my feet by the next heartbreaker in sheep's clothing. I was so consistently unlucky in love that, by the age of 26, I was starting to believe I might be cursed. It felt like I was doomed to forever wander the Earth, attracting every flakey, unreliable man within a 50-mile radius, along with all the gaslighters and cheaters to boot.

For most of my early twenties, the tragic state of my love life was baffling to me. How had I seemingly become a beacon for all the wrong sorts of men? Why, when I dreamed so longingly of a Disney-style happily-ever-after, did I always seem to end up with the villain? Now that I have a little more age and wisdom on my side (not to mention several professional opinions that I paid through the nose for), I can pinpoint the exact moment that set me up for all those years of disastrous dating. It was the moment I got romantically entangled with my very first boyfriend at the age of 17.

In our circle of friends, Matt scooped up the titles of most charming, most charismatic, funniest, most eloquent, and most likely to walk into a room full of strangers and immediately befriend everyone. Even then, when we were all so young and still as socially awkward as Bambi on ice, he somehow effortlessly balanced unwavering confidence with a quirky, likeable humility. He was tall, handsome, funny, and generous. And I … had no interest in him.

I had no interest in being in a relationship at all. Life was just beginning to bloom with adventures and opportunities, and finding a boyfriend wasn't a priority for me. I explained that to Matt when he told me that he had feelings for me. I told him again and again over the course of the next few months, but he kept bouncing back with a persistence that seemed sweet.

Then, one crisp, autumnal evening, when a group of us were gathered around a bonfire, he called me over to where he was sitting. He looked up at me out of the corner of his eyes and flashed a cheeky grin.

"I give up," he said with a shrug. "I'm not asking anymore, Aimée. From now on, I'm just going to start calling you my girlfriend – whether you like it or not."

It must have seemed awfully romantic at that moment because, rather than objecting, my teenage self simply blushed and went along with the whole thing. Now I can see that it wasn't a cute, romantic moment – it was an enormous red flag.

You see, once upon a time – back when Blackberrys were the height of cool and Tinchy Stryder was in the charts – I dated a narcissist. I was young, utterly clueless when it came to relationships, and genuinely believed I was in love with the guy. Spoiler alert: it wasn't love. It was a mess.

In the beginning, the whole thing really did have the air of the fairytale romance I'd been dreaming of. Matt treated me like I was the focal point of his entire world. He'd whisper compliments in my ear and bring me flowers. My friends would gush over the charming things he'd say about me and, when he'd look at me, his face would be filled with so much emotion that it made me blush.

After only a few short weeks of this whirlwind romance, he told me he loved me.

"Really?" I almost choked in reply. Wasn't love supposed to be a momentous, life-altering, all-consuming event? Was he already there, after just a few short weeks? Was I?

"Of course," he said, flashing me a smile. He picked up my hand and squeezed my fingers gently. "You're incredible! You're the girl I want to be with forever. I can't imagine my life without you." A note of expectancy hung awkwardly in the air.

"Oh," I said, taking a few seconds to process the situation. If he was already so sure that he was in love with me, then why didn't I feel the same way?

Maybe … I am in love.

I mean, I guess … Why not?

"I love you, too," I said finally. It tumbled out with a flat note of uncertainty that he didn't seem to notice.

Every part of our relationship was intense – the way he looked at me, the way he called me by my full name, the way he held my hand tightly in his wherever we went. Red flag. Red flag. Red flag. But this was the *Twilight* era. My only reference points for what a healthy relationship should look like were my monthly copy of *Cosmopolitan* and a romance novel about a vampire whose greatest desire is to kill his girlfriend. It's no wonder I didn't see the warning signs. I never thought to wonder why this guy who barely knew me suddenly acted as though I was his entire world. I was just flattered to hear him say he couldn't live without me.

Then, as the months went by, it became apparent that he really couldn't live without me. Rather, he wouldn't. He struggled to spend any time apart from me. If I made plans with my friends that didn't include him, he'd beg me to cancel. Gradually, that begging shifted into ordering. His loving compliments dissolved into irritated jibes, raised voices, and snide remarks. On the nights when I was too tired to drive over to his house to visit him, he'd berate me over the phone until I gave in, grabbed my keys, and made the drive in the dark with tears sliding down my face. On the rare occasions when I went out with my girlfriends, he'd turn up out of the blue to surprise me.

My once tight-knit support system of friends slowly began to unravel. Their days of applauding me on my sweet, doting boyfriend were over. Now, he just made them feel uncomfortable. There were some friends I was outright banned from seeing and, on the days when I would slip away to spend time with them in secret, my exhausted heart would pound in my chest every time I got a text message. I was terrified he'd spot me there, or even

they don't offer some kind of post-toxic-relationship-exorcism for this kind of thing.

So, instead of happily-ever-after, I found myself in an assortment of grim, short-lived relationships instead. Each new disastrous attempt at love just reinforced all those negative beliefs that were worming their way through my subconscious mind. It was a self-perpetuating cycle that I wouldn't even become aware of – let alone begin to dismantle – until I was nearly 30. Until then, I flitted hopelessly from one heartbreak to the next.

Let me introduce you to the cast of my cataclysmic love life:

There was the guy who fell asleep during our breakup.

Then there was the guy who told me he loved me, only to tell me two weeks later that, actually, he'd changed his mind and I was just "okay".

There was the guy who had me take out a loan so I could visit him in Germany, just so he could tell me he didn't want to date me anymore.

Let's not forget the guy with the secret wife and children.

But there was the guy who broke the cycle. This man filled my world with such genuine love and kindness that it tipped my world upside down. And then he broke my heart so completely that it broke the whole of me, shattered me to the core, and tore my entire life apart.

I know what you're thinking ... *Girl, that is intense! What is this* – The Notebook?

The truth is, this is the story of a gut-wrenching, soul-destroying, cry-until-you-physically-vomit type of heartbreak. That's okay, though, because, as counter-intuitive as it may seem, it's ultimately a happy story. Yes, it's a story filled with heartache, but it's also the story of a girl who got torn apart and then collected all the broken pieces and built herself back up, stronger. It's a story of resilience, healing, growth, and, above all else, self-love.

PART ONE:

Happily Ever Temporarily

Chapter 1

I was nearly nine years into my disastrous dating streak when I met Dylan. It seemed like Fate. Actually, it seemed like Fate had twisted my arm, given me a good shove in his direction, and forced me into it. Fate and I weren't on very good terms for a long time after that.

I was 27 years old and I had just moved to Bahrain, a tiny jewel of an island in the Persian Gulf. A haphazard series of events had led me there. For the last few years, I had bounced from one thing to another with the erratic energy of a ball spinning around inside a pinball machine. I was searching for something. I had no idea what it was or how to find it. The only thing I knew for sure was that the nagging, empty sensation I felt was growing and I simply had to find a way to fill it.

So, not long after my 25th birthday, I left my stable, responsible, grown-up, corporate job. I handed in the keys to my flashy company car and closed the door on the lavish parties in London and impressive monthly salary.

Without so much as a flicker of doubt crossing my mind, I walked away from all of the things people told me should make me happy in pursuit of something that really would.

I had no plan, but the determination to fill that void kept pushing me forwards. In the space of the next two years, I retrained as a teacher, accepted a job offer in Kuwait, moved my entire life to a part of the world I knew barely anything about, and spent an entire summer travelling southeast Asia (meditating with monks, playing with elephants – the whole shebang).

Somehow, I thrived in the chaos of it all, and I was unquestionably happier. But, whatever it was that was missing, I still hadn't found it. That strange sense of emptiness was still gnawing away at me in the background. When my teaching contract came up for renewal in Kuwait, I decided to relocate again. That's how I ended up in Bahrain. It seemed as good a place as any to search for this missing puzzle piece, not least because there's no income tax and there are some really nice rooftop cocktail bars there.

It didn't take long for me to settle into my new life in Bahrain. After just a few days, that little island felt like home. It was so beautiful with its vibrant, turquoise waters and long, dusty-orange sunsets that lit up the evening sky against the silhouette of the minarets. Even the crowded streets that buzzed with the sound of traffic and the dusty, grey expanses that punctuated more built-up parts of the city seemed oddly charming. I loved how every day seemed to beam with a burst of brilliant sunshine and the promise of my own mini-adventure. Sure, I wasn't a huge fan of the early morning call to prayer on the weekends, but you can't have everything.

It helped that I didn't move there alone. My best friend, Nina, had decided to relocate with me. Nina and I had met the year before in Kuwait. We'd both taught at the same international school and had clicked on the very first day. I'd stood in the lobby with the other new teachers, glancing nervously out into the sea of unfamiliar faces. Nina's head had popped up above the others and she'd struck up an enthusiastic conversation with me from across the room, raising her voice unashamedly above the polite-yet-strained mumble of small talk from the others. We became friends immediately and clung to each other through the highs and lows of ex-pat life and the stresses of teaching abroad.

Our personalities meshed together perfectly to form an inevitable friendship. In a lot of ways, we were practically the same personality split between two bodies. We shared everything, from interests and political ideologies to clothes and trips to far-flung destinations. We laughed at the same stupid jokes that nobody else found funny. There was nothing I could say to Nina that she wouldn't immediately understand, as if the thought had come out of her own head instead of mine. In time, we didn't even need to say anything. We could communicate with each other across a crowded room with a series of meaningful glances.

But, for all our similarities, we were also polar opposites. When I zigged, Nina zagged. If I began to think too deeply about a problem and stress myself out, Nina was able to step back and think things through logically and stoically. When Nina would whizz off into a world of her own and throw caution to the wind, I would help her navigate reality. We balanced each other out perfectly. There was never a mean comment or raised voice between us and, on the nights when we drank one glass of wine too many, we'd declare to anyone who would listen that we were "non-romantic soulmates".

When I told Nina that I was planning on moving to Bahrain, her immediate response was, "I'll come too!" I was thrilled. Her only condition was that we find an apartment that we could share because, as she pointed out, we would have more fun as roommates than we possibly could living alone.

We found the perfect apartment on our second day in Bahrain. After sifting through pages of apartment listings in Nina's hotel room for a few hours, we found a building that we fell in love with.

"It's only a few blocks away," Nina said, zooming in on the map. "We could go there now."

"Can you just turn up to an apartment building and say, 'Hey, we'd like an apartment please?'" I asked sceptically. Nina shrugged.

"It's worth a try."

As it turns out, in Bahrain you can just turn up to an apartment building and say, "Hey, we'd like an apartment, please?" Within the space of two hours, we'd found the building, chosen an apartment, and signed the lease. It was our dream home.

It was bright and modern, with tall, spacious rooms and fancy amenities. We had access to a private pool, cinema, and gym. From our balcony, the city below melted into a balmy haze, and in the evenings, we could sit with a glass of wine and watch the world light up in the darkness. Plus, we had the kinds of built-in closets that dreams are made of. I felt like the Carrie Bradshaw of the Gulf region.

Our new apartment was in Juffair, a bustling city on the northeast coast of the island. The US Navy has an enormous base there and, consequently, the city is full of fun cocktail bars, nightclubs, and American-style restaurants. Just one street over from our apartment building was a street affectionately nicknamed "American Alley" because it was so crammed with western chain restaurants. At night, the neon lights from the likes of McDonald's, TGI Fridays, and Dunkin' Donuts gleamed in the balmy darkness.

Juffair is nothing like the other areas of Bahrain. It doesn't have the fancy sparkle of Amwaj with its private beaches, or the prestige of Riffa with its luxurious homes fit for royalty. In fact, a lot of people refer to Juffair as "tacky". Taken at surface value, with its sheer volume of cheap nightclubs, fast-food restaurants, and sex workers, it's easy to see why some people may feel that way. When you look a little closer, though, you see that the busy city built around the military base has a strangely charming meshing of cultures.

On any given street, you'll see a man in a traditional thawb pass someone sporting a pair of cowboy boots. The air there is filled with the sound of the call to prayer mingled with the distant music of Florida Georgie Line. American-style BBQ houses can be found on most corners, with the caveat that the bacon is usually pork-free. It's a city unlike anywhere else, and it will always hold a special place in my heart.

Aside from the sheer quirkiness of it, my favourite thing about living in Juffair was the social life. Swarming with ex-pats, it was the best part of the island to meet new people. It was the kind of place where you could walk into a bar and strike up a conversation with anyone. In fact, Nina and I had only been in the country for just under a week when we met a man who would ultimately become one of my most cherished friends.

That night, we were sitting upstairs in JJ's, our favourite Irish pub. It was a large space decorated with dark wooden floors and furniture. The doors and parts of the walls were painted matte black, and the low, unflattering lighting cast strange shadows across the stained floors. There were startlingly bright pops of leprechaun green scattered throughout, though I'm not sure if that was in an attempt to brighten the feel of the place or to remind customers of the pub's Irish origin. Either way, it all looked very unseemly, but somehow still radiated a welcoming air.

We were sitting at a table off to the side, chatting about our new jobs and our first impressions of Bahrain. Near the stairs was a table full of young, rambunctious American men. They were laughing and whooping as one of them popped the cork out of a bottle of champagne. I watched with an interested smile as they toasted and cheered. They were all wearing suits, and it was clear from their loud laughter and glazed expressions that this was not their first stop of the evening.

Nina and I continued our conversation and, out of the corner of my eye, I watched one of the men break away from the group and start working his way around the pub, from one table to the next. He'd collapse into the nearest chair and strike up a conversation with the people at the table for a few moments before getting (rather unsteadily) to his feet again and moving on to the next one. Eventually, it was our turn.

He slumped down into the chair next to me and looked from Nina to me.

"Hi," he said.

This man, we would learn, was Nick, a blond-haired giant of a New Yorker with a booming voice that threatens to shake the window panes when he laughed. He also has a heart of absolute gold.

"Are you guys having a good night?" I nodded over to the table by the stairs where Nick's friends had started their own dance party.

"Yeah!" he said enthusiastically. "It's my birthday!"

"Happy birthday!" Nina and I said simultaneously. Nick smiled and thanked us in a voice that was starting to slur.

"Here's the deal," he said suddenly, trying to rearrange his face into a serious expression. He banged his enormous palms on the table in front of him. "Do you guys … want some fries?" The odd question hung in the air for a moment before Nina answered.

"Umm … No, thank you."

Nick rolled his eyes in frustration and his whole head rolled around with them. "C'mon! We ordered all these baskets of fries, and it's too many. We can't eat them all." Nina and I just stared at him, slightly taken aback by his passion for the subject. "Someone needs to eat the fries!" he said, throwing his arms in the air.

"Okay," Nina laughed. "We'll eat some."

"Thank you!" He got up out of the chair and headed back to his table. Nina and I exchanged an amused look and then he was back. He tossed a basket of fries onto the table with a satisfied grin.

"Thank you," we said.

I'm still not entirely sure how, but that drunken offering of a basket of fries led to the formation of one of the most important and long-lasting friendships I made in Bahrain.

The three of us just clicked and, before long, Nick became like an unofficial third roommate who could come and go as he pleased. Some days I would get back to the apartment building after work, and I would know he was there before the elevator doors even opened. His thunderous laugh would echo through the corridors and right down the elevator shaft.

Nick made us laugh so much, we'd be curled up on the sofa, gasping for air. He would fix our broken appliances (most of which weren't actually broken – we just couldn't figure out how to use them), and he was the one we went to for advice about life in Bahrain. It was Nick we called the night a driver locked us in his taxi, refusing to let us out, and Nick whom we screamed down the phone to in terror when we were convinced there was a ghost in our apartment. He was our hero.

He was also a social butterfly. It seemed as though he knew every single person living on the island and, if he ever came across someone he didn't know, he was always quick to introduce himself and instantly gain another friend. He introduced Nina and me to practically every person and every place in Juffair. We couldn't walk into a bar or restaurant without someone calling out, "Hey, it's Nick!" with a grin.

Actually, looking back, I think every single friendship or acquaintance I made (outside of work) for the full two years that I lived in Bahrain can be traced back to an introduction made by Nick. Needless to say, my experience there wouldn't have been the same whirlwind of adventures if he hadn't been a part of it.

Overall, within those first few months of my new life in Bahrain, everything seemed to slot into place surprisingly effortlessly. It just felt right. I loved waking up each morning like a starfish spread out in my enormous bed. I loved the evenings Nina and I spent gossiping over wine in our living room. I loved each new place we visited, each restaurant we ate at, and each cocktail bar we tried. For a girl who grew up in a small town in South Wales where, for a while, the biggest attraction was the new Burger King on the beachfront, Bahrain seemed like a place of endless adventures and places to explore. Finally, I was starting to feel a sense of peace. That nagging sense of discontentment had eased. I was happy.

I barely had time to sink into my new routine before I was met with another huge change, though. The excitement of moving had barely even settled when I first met Dylan, and suddenly my entire life was thrown up into disarray again.

Chapter 2

I wasn't supposed to be there that night. The night that Dylan and I first met, I'd wanted to stay in the apartment. I had no desire to wrestle my hair into submission, put on a pretty dress, and go out into the world. Nina, on the other hand, was desperate to go out dancing.

"You'll have so much fun when we get there!" she said.

I was already in my pyjamas with my damp hair scraped back into a bun, midway through a Netflix show and a chocolate-covered crepe.

"The last time we went there it was full of creepy men," I reminded her.

"It might be different this time," she said, although she didn't sound convinced.

When we'd first moved to Bahrain, Vibe had been our favourite club, but just two months later, it was already starting to show the early signs of a quick and definite decline. A lot of bars and clubs in Bahrain seemed to have a very limited lifespan. They would become popular almost overnight, attracting all the same faces I was used to seeing around the city. Then, just as suddenly, they would peak and descend into a state of squalor and anonymity. It was a strange cycle that I never quite got used to, and it meant you could never let yourself get too attached to any hangout.

"I don't want to go out," I groaned. "I don't want to be around people. I don't want to be in the same space as men."

I was in no mood for dancing that night. Nor was I interested in stepping foot outside of the apartment for the rest of my life. The night that I met Dylan, I was still berating myself over my most recent dating mishap. Things had ended abruptly (and dramatically) between me and the marine I'd been seeing. It had all seemed to be going so well, right until the night he'd invited me out dancing. We'd walked into the club together, laughing and smiling and then, as soon as we reached the dancefloor, he'd dropped my hand to grab another girl's arse. I was so shocked that all I could do was stare in horrified disbelief as my date started grinding on another woman a few feet away from me.

I was still recovering from the sheer shock and humiliation of it all the next morning when my friend Mason hit me with the news that it was all irrelevant anyway, because my marine had a wife and two children back in Michigan.

"He's not married!" I insisted, but there was a sinking sensation in my stomach. My words didn't come out with the conviction I'd expected them to. We were eating a takeaway breakfast in the living room. Mason was devouring his bagel with enthusiasm, but mine remained untouched.

"Yes, he is," Mason said simply. He took another bite of his breakfast, while I stared up at him in silence, trying to process this new blow.

"He doesn't have a wedding ring," I said eventually.

Mason shrugged. "He's on deployment. Most of the guys in my battalion took off their wedding rings before the plane even left the tarmac." He pointed his bagel at me suddenly and gave me a serious look. "You can't tell anyone I told you that, though. 'Bros before hoes' is one of the most important things they teach you in basic training, right after marksmanship."

"So …" I said slowly, succumbing to the inevitable realisation that, once again, I'd walked straight into another man-trap. "You're telling me that I dated somebody else's husband?"

Mason glanced over at my face, which was twisted into an expression of horror and disgust. He momentarily lowered his bagel.

"It's not like you knew he was married, though," he said, trying to be helpful.

"What's wrong with me?" I cried, tossing my breakfast to one side and planting my face in the nearest pillow. "Why do I always pick the worst types of men?"

This most recent stain on my already-messy dating record was enough to convince me that it was time to give men a wide berth for a while. It wasn't even the complete lack of respect this guy had shown me or the fact that he had so unashamedly cheated on his wife that led me to this conclusion. It was that, somehow, I'd managed to convince myself that it was all my fault. I'd sifted through the chain of events in my mind and decided that all of this man's lying, cheating, and selfish behaviours were a reflection of my inadequacies, instead of his.

After all, you never specifically asked him outright if he was married, did you?

I'd sat, stunned, when that thought first echoed through my mind. Immediately, I knew I was wrong to blame myself for his actions. Even so, I couldn't silence the whispers in the back of my head that insisted that this was somehow my fault – that I deserved it. What's more, this most recent development had shaken loose the outer shell of happiness I'd been feeling since I'd moved to Bahrain and revealed that the unsettling, empty feeling was still lurking underneath it all.

Okay. No more dating for you until you figure out exactly what is going on with that.

So I hadn't wanted to go out that night. I'd wanted to mope around in my man-free apartment and eat myself into a sugar-induced coma.

"You can wear my black skirt," Nina said.

I rolled my eyes and stuffed a huge bite of crepe into my mouth.

"Fine!"

When we got to Vibe, the bouncer stuffed a wad of free drinks coupons into our hands and ushered us inside. The dancefloor was empty and pockets of people were milling around near the bar and over by the pool tables. That night it most certainly was not a vibe.

We handed over our coupons at the bar and surveyed the scene. I couldn't pick out a single face I recognised.

"Is it me," Nina shouted over the thud of the music, "or are there a lot of very creepy men here tonight?" She looked pointedly to our left, where a small group of men were huddled near the bar, staring intently in our direction. I took a sip of my cheap whiskey and shuddered.

"Why did you bring me here?" I laughed.

"Come on," Nina said, giggling too. She grabbed my hand and pulled me into the centre of the dancefloor. I sipped my drink and danced half-heartedly with robotic movements. My mind was already floating away elsewhere. I was just beginning to wonder about my disastrous dating history again when a man bounded over from the other side of the dancefloor and stopped dead right in front of me.

I looked up at him and blinked, a little taken aback by his sudden appearance. He was broad-shouldered and square-jawed with dark eyes that looked at me from a face arranged into a nervous expression.

"Can I have your number?" he shouted over the noise of the music.

That was it. No introduction or attempt at a pick-up line. No conversation of any sort. Just this big, drunk American guy who looked like a real-life GI Joe, standing in front of me, holding his phone in front of my face. He flashed me a shy yet expectant smile. Usually, I don't give my number out to drunken strangers, and this rule was meant to be even more iron-clad than ever, now that I was officially boycotting dating. But there was just something so immediately charming about this man that, before I stopped to make sense of what I was doing, I found myself typing my number into his phone. I was partially convinced by his cute, crooked smile, but mostly I was just thrown off-guard by the sheer suddenness of it all. I handed his phone back to him and waited for an introduction. He flashed me another smile.

"Thanks!" he said, and turned on his heels and walked away.

I stared after him, wondering what on earth had just happened.

"What was that about?" Nina shouted over at me.

"He wanted my number," I said. My eyebrows were screwed up in confusion.

"And you gave it to him?" Nina said in surprise. "What's his name?"

"I have absolutely no idea," I told her.

And in that one small, bizarre moment, the entire trajectory of my life changed.

For the next three nights, Dylan texted me, asking me out to various parties or get-togethers with his friends. In fact, he was so enthusiastic and seemed so determined to get me to turn up to these events, that I started to wonder if maybe he was a serial killer.

"He just likes you!" Nina said, rolling her eyes.

"You don't think it's weird that he just happens to have a party to invite me to every single night of the week?"

"He's in the military!" she said, exasperated. "You know those guys love to party! Please tell him we'll go to the party tonight."

We were perched on precarious stools at the bar in JJ's. It was a Sunday evening, the most fun-drained day of the week because, in Bahrain, Friday and Saturday make up the weekend. For that reason, the bar was, unsurprisingly, empty. The sound of a football game droned from the huge TV on the wall. Two men sat at a table towards the back of the room, transfixed by whatever was happening on the screen. They were the only other people there.

I glanced down at my phone where Dylan's most recent message was waiting for a response. Then I looked back up at Nina's pleading face.

"Please!" she said. "It's so boring here tonight."

"Okay, fine! But if we end up dead, it's your fault."

I sent Dylan a text, asking for the address of that night's party, and told him we'd order an Uber from JJ's. I got an immediate response.

Dylan: *Oh great! Don't worry about ordering an Uber. I'll get it.*

I raised my eyes in surprise. No man had ever offered to pay for my Uber ride before. Sure, if he really was a serial killer, then he was potentially paying for a one-way ticket to my brutal murder, but it still surpassed most of the things any other man had done for me in the past. I broke out into a small smile in spite of myself.

Half an hour later, our Uber pulled up at the end of a cul-de-sac a few blocks away from our apartment building. Three huge, white villas were spread out across the dusty, grey road. Nina and I climbed out of the car and looked around. The street was dark and quiet. The Uber did a quick U-turn and headed back to the centre of the city, leaving us standing awkwardly in the middle of the road, alone and unsure of what to do next.

"See?" I said, turning to Nina. "This is where we get murdered."

Before she had a chance to respond, we heard the sound of clanking metal to our left. A tall gate swung open and let light spill out onto the street. There was Dylan, drink in hand, with a huge smile on his face.

"You made it!" He ushered us in and closed the gate behind us. "What do you girls want to drink?" he asked as we made our way into the house. The huge, open-plan living area was filled with people. Some were dancing in the middle of the living room; some were playing a particularly passionate game of beer-pong in the kitchen; and others were spread out, talking and laughing loudly above the blare of the music. The air was thick with the smell of vodka. Clearly, this party had been going on for a while already.

"I'll have a gin and tonic," said Nina.

"Can I have a Jack and Diet Coke please?" I asked. I was still looking around and taking in the scene. Dylan stopped in his tracks so suddenly that I almost walked straight into the back of him. He spun around and stared at me with a wide-eyed expression.

"A Jack Daniel's with Diet Coke?" he repeated, still staring at me.

I smiled, awkwardly. No one expects a five-foot-three British girl to ask for whiskey, but I'd never had a reaction quite this extreme to my drink order before.

"Yeah," I said slowly. "Do you … have Jack Daniel's?" I asked.

"Of course!" Dylan said, breaking into a sudden smile. "Oh my God. I think you're my dream girl!"

And I really think I was his dream girl. I certainly was that night, and for many nights after that, anyway. But the unfortunate reality is that dreams can change. Sometimes priorities shift, and the things that used to seem so incredible suddenly don't shine quite as brightly anymore.

Nina disappeared into the crowd and started mingling. I took a seat opposite Dylan, and we began chatting.

"So you're in the military?" I asked.

"Who told you that?" Dylan looked shocked. "I mean, it's not something I tell people when I first meet them. A lot of people make assumptions about you when they find out you're in the military."

"Well, you're an American living in Juffair, so I'd say your cover is pretty much blown," I laughed.

"I didn't think of that," he said, chuckling too. "I've only been here for a few weeks."

The hours slipped away and we stayed glued in that little corner of the room, oblivious for the most part to all of the carnage going on around us. We chatted about work and where we'd grown up. We cradled our whiskeys that were probably too strong for a work night, and I struggled to decide if it was the alcohol that was making me feel so giddy or if it was Dylan.

Maybe it was the way he listened so intently as I spoke, fixing his kind eyes on me. Maybe it was the way the conversation flowed so naturally between us, nearly as easily as the drinks did. Maybe it was just a case of undeniable magnetic attraction. Whatever it was, I felt myself warming to him almost instantly.

You're supposed to be boycotting men, remember?

"Okay," Dylan said, setting his glass down on the table in front of us. He fixed me with as serious an expression as his current state of sobriety allowed. "I want you to know that I'm wearing these sweatpants because one of the guys pushed me in the pool and now my jeans are in the washing machine." He gestured to the baggy, grey sweatpants he was wearing with an apologetic grimace.

I was trying my hardest to stay aloof and not let myself get drawn in, but I couldn't help giggling into my glass of Jack Daniel's.

"You've actually already apologised for your sweatpants three times already," I told him. "And you don't need to apologise anyway. It's your house. You can wear whatever you want."

"Have I?" He laughed. "I'm sorry. I guess I'm a little buzzed. I just don't want you to think that I think that I look cool … Do you know what I mean? I know I look ridiculous."

"You don't look ridiculous."

"No, I do and I don't want you to think I'm this weird sweatpants guy."

"I don't," I assured him, still laughing. "I promise."

He stared straight into my eyes again. I took a quick sip of my drink and dragged my gaze away from his. I could sense that he was still looking at me.

"I …" He fumbled around for the words for a moment. "I really want to kiss you right now."

My head snapped back up in surprise. I looked at him and shook my head.

"I barely know you," I said with a smile. "So I don't think that would be a good idea."

Besides, didn't you say you weren't even going near another man for the foreseeable future because you need to work on your self-esteem?

Shut up! I am totally in control of this situation.

"You're right," Dylan said and he apologised. "I just … there's something about you. And … you're really beautiful," he stammered. Suddenly he sounded a little nervous.

I looked back down into my lap. For some reason, I was nervous, too.

"Thank you," I said, trying my best to ignore the uncomfortable tingling sensation in my fingers.

You are not *in control of this situation. Stop this now. You're meant to be working on yourself, remember?*

"I'd like to take you out on a date," Dylan said. He was looking over at me with an adorable expression of hopeful anticipation that made me smile.

"Yeah, I'd like that," I said, and ignored everything within me that screamed that this was a terrible mistake.

Chapter 3

I had no intention of falling in love with this man. In fact, I fought it with every fibre of my being. After my most recent humiliation at the hands of the lying, cheating marine I'd been so convinced was a catch, I knew I needed to work through some issues.

Firstly, my judgement when it came to men was clearly off. Why was I always blind to the carnival of red flags waving wildly in front of my eyes? Then there was the way I reacted to being treated so disrespectfully. Rather, the way I didn't react. When I rooted through my memories, I found countless instances in which former boyfriends had said awful things to me or treated me as if I simply didn't matter. I'd never stuck up for myself. I'd never felt hurt or angry. In fact, it had never even registered that the things they were saying and doing were wrong. I'd simply glossed over them and stored each occurrence away in some dark recess of my mind, unexamined.

Apparently, the ordeal with the marine had been the final straw. All of a sudden, these past thoughts and experiences had been forced to the surface and, as I began sifting through it all, I recognised a pattern. I was finally able to see that none of this was normal and that, somewhere along the way, I'd lost all sense of what was acceptable and what wasn't. My self-esteem was shattered, and I was weighed down with feelings of self-doubt and inadequacy. For years, I'd let people waltz into my life and treat me with complete disregard because deep down I didn't think I deserved any better. Each new, dysfunctional relationship just reinforced those beliefs. I'd been caught up in a cruel cycle, and I'd never even realised it until now.

On the outside, I seemed confident. I had no qualms about travelling the world alone, speaking in front of a roomful of people, or plastering my life all over social media for everyone to see. The facade of this self-assured young woman who didn't care what other people thought had been so convincing that even I'd believed it. It was only when I peeked behind the outer exterior that I realised how frail the foundations were.

I needed time to work through that jumbled mess and fix my broken thoughts. I needed to learn to respect myself and set healthy boundaries. Most of all, I needed to avoid any more rejection until I'd done those things. Deep down,

I knew that another rejection might tip my already fragile sense of self-worth over the edge. What I needed most at that time was to be alone and to focus on myself.

Instead, I went on that date with Dylan.

I convinced myself it was going to be casual. I wore jeans, a little pink camisole, and a white lace cardigan. Casual. I didn't do winged eyeliner. Casual. It's just a date, nothing more. Casual!

What I didn't realise was that, by handing over my phone number that night in the club, I'd unwittingly stepped into the wrestling ring with Fate. Over the next few months, I fought my hardest. I kicked. I screamed. I clung to the ropes for dear life, but in the end, there was no escaping the fact that this was going to be anything but casual.

It was clear from that very first date that Dylan was nothing like any of the other guys I'd dated before. He came to my apartment to pick me up for dinner and his face lit up with a nervous smile when I opened the door. I was hit with another debilitating wave of nervousness. Something about him just knocked all of the sense right out of my head.

"I've never been to this place," he told me as we headed downstairs to meet our Uber. "But I remember you said you're vegetarian, so I tried to find somewhere that would have lots of options for you to choose from."

"Thank you," I said with a surprised smile. "You didn't need to go to so much effort." He looked a little confused and laughed.

"I wouldn't want to take you somewhere where you couldn't eat anything," he said. "I remember you saying you like Italian food …"

"It's my favourite!"

"Mine too!"

When we pulled up outside the little Italian restaurant in the next city over, he rushed to open my car door for me. He pulled out the chair for me when we sat down at our table. He asked me questions about myself as we munched on bread from the basket in the centre of the table and listened with undistracted interest. Then, after we'd stuffed ourselves full with delicious pasta, he snatched the bill off the table before I could even glance at it.

"I can pay half," I assured him, and he looked almost offended.

"I wouldn't invite you out for dinner and then expect you to pay," he told me.

Throughout the evening, he was sweet, attentive, and kind. As he rushed to hold the Uber door open for me again on the way home, I began to wonder if somehow I'd stumbled on a true, honest gentleman. Was this the Prince Charming I'd been waiting for?

"I'll walk you up to your apartment," he said as the Uber pulled up outside my building. With those words, the dream of old-fashioned chivalry crumbled into pieces.

"You really don't have to," I told him, trying to hide my disappointment.

He'd seemed so genuinely nice. He'd said and done all the loveliest things all evening. Now he was going to try to edge his way into my apartment, shattering the facade of a man who had any kind of good intentions.

"I'd really feel better knowing I got you home safe," he insisted.

We rode up to the eleventh floor in the elevator and I could feel a fresh wave of nervousness building in the pit of my stomach.

What's the polite way of telling someone, "You can't come in"?

We stood outside the apartment and I fumbled for my keys in my bag, waiting with tensed shoulders for the inevitable awkwardness of it all.

"Thank you so much," I said, glancing up at him. "I had a really nice time."

"Me too," he said with another nervous smile. He opened his mouth and I braced myself. "May I … kiss you?"

I looked up at him, shocked. That wasn't the question I'd been expecting.

"Yes," I said, still a little taken aback. He leaned down and lightly brushed his lips against mine for just a few seconds. It was the sweetest kiss of my life.

"I'll text you when I get home," he said with a beaming smile. Then he turned on his heels and headed back down the corridor.

I stared after him, still in a state of surprise. He hadn't tried to get into my apartment. He hadn't said a single impolite word to me all night. He didn't even try to jam his tongue down my throat when he kissed me. Instead, he'd taken me for a lovely meal that he'd planned around my tastes, and he'd had spent the evening complimenting me and treating me with the utmost respect. I didn't quite know what to make of it. After all, for years, the closest thing I'd had to a first date was a late-night text message saying, *"Come to JJ's."*

This is too good to be true. You're going to get hurt.

Dylan and I went on three more dates, and throughout each one, I struggled to ignore the voice in the back of my head that was frantically begging me not to get too attached to this man. I felt torn. I knew I needed to be alone and work on myself. There were deep cracks in the foundations of myself that I needed to fix before I even thought about getting into another relationship. I was opening myself up for potential devastation. All of this was undeniable. But tearing myself away from Dylan's company already felt impossible.

And that's exactly why it's so important that you do it!

One Friday afternoon a group of us gathered in the apartment to eat our weight in takeaway food and watch *Les Miserables*. I glanced over at Dylan continuously as France descended into revolutionary chaos, preparing myself for the conversation I didn't want to have. I pulled him to one side as everyone was leaving and took a deep breath, sorting through the words in my mind before I said them out loud.

"I think you're a really amazing guy," I said and I watched as his shoulders sag with realisation. "And I love spending time with you. I know it's going to sound cheesy and clichéd, but this just isn't a good time for me to get into a relationship. Like … really."

He nodded with a sad smile and I looked down at the floor.

"It's fine," he told me. "We can just be friends instead."

As it turned out, we could not be friends instead. We could be two people who hung out together at every given opportunity. We could be two people with in-jokes who bonded over music and movies. We could even be two people who kept strictly platonic boundaries physically. But we were not friends. Friends don't feel that thrilling spark of electricity when their hands accidentally brush against each other. Their hearts don't jump in their chests when they see the other person walk into a room. Friends don't feel the way about each other that we felt.

Slowly but surely, the promise I'd made to myself to hide my heart away from anyone who might break it melted into mush. As the months wore on, our faux-platonic relationship became more and more complicated, more and more strained. Aside from the fact that I was still in no fit state to embark on a new relationship, there was no way that Dylan and I could make it work anyway. He would be leaving Bahrain for work in just a few months and it would be a long time before he'd be back. There was simply no plausible way that we could be together.

The issue was that by this time, there was also no plausible way for us to be apart. I'd tried for months to peel myself away from him, to build up a wall between us, to convince myself to walk away, but I couldn't.

"We can't do this," I cried down the phone at him one night. I was sitting in the dark on my bedroom floor and tears were dropping into my lap. "You're going to leave soon and if I let myself fall for you, it's going to break my heart."

"I know," he said, his voice strained with emotion. "But I haven't felt this way about anyone in so long. I can't stop thinking about you."

"We have to end this," I said, wiping tears from my eyes. "We've tried being friends and it doesn't work. We just have to completely stay away from each other."

"I don't want to do that," he pleaded.

"I don't want to do it either, but we have to."

I sobbed as we both reluctantly agreed to cut all contact and do our best to simply forget each other.

It lasted a day.

The next morning, I went to bottomless brunch with Nina, Nick, and Mason at a fancy hotel on the other side of the island. There were trays and trays filled with delicious foods to choose from, an entire tower of desserts, and plenty of different cocktails on offer. I tried to force down the sadness with tequila, and fill up the empty space with half a dozen tiny cheesecakes. I joined in with my friends as they laughed over their drinks and whirled around the dancefloor. Deep down, I felt empty.

No matter how many aesthetically pleasing desserts I nibbled on or how strong I had the bartender mix my margaritas, there was no pleasure in any of it. All afternoon, I felt my eyes wandering towards the door, as if, by some miracle, Dylan would suddenly appear in the entryway. I picked up and put down my phone over and over again. There were never any new messages.

Don't you dare text him! You've done the right thing.

The day wore on. I sipped at my cocktails and joined in with The Cupid Shuffle, but my heart just wasn't in it. When brunch finally came to an end and everyone suggested we finish off the evening at JJ's, I gave a reluctant smile and clambered into the Uber, wishing I could just go home and crawl into bed instead. Looking back, it's strange how so many of my monumental life events have taken place in that dingy, little Irish pub. That night, it was there that Fate cornered me once again and seemed to yell above the thick clouds of cigarette smoke and the booming of the music, "You think you can walk away that easily? Really?"

The bar was packed that night. As we walked in, we had to squeeze through a cluster of people gathered around the bar. The dancefloor was full of people, springing around with reckless abandon and drinking in the joy of the weekend. The sickly smell of Jaeger mingled with stale smoke clung to the walls. Even in the low light, it was clear that every table was full. The sounds of drunken laughter and conversation were swallowed up by the blare of the live band on stage.

The bartender poured our regular drinks, and Nina pulled me onto the dancefloor, through the throng of people. Nick and Mason followed, and all three of them began dancing wildly to the music. Again, I felt my eyes wandering, scanning the room for any sign of Dylan in among the heaving Friday-night crowd. There was no sign of him, and I felt simultaneously disappointed and relieved.

"Come on!" Nick yelled over the noise. He grabbed my hands and spun me around. I laughed and started dancing, trying to resist the urge to survey the room again.

Eventually, the band retired, and the familiar announcement came on over the speakers that curfew was about to begin. In Bahrain, all members of the US military have to clear out of the bars at midnight. It's like a sloppier, more tequila-fuelled version of *Cinderella*. The doors opened and people began to empty out onto the street. I booked an Uber and headed outside to wait with Nina.

That's when I saw him, looking just as regretful and miserable as I was feeling. I caught a glimpse of him as I walked out onto the pavement. He was standing a little way down the street with a group of his friends and he didn't see me. Nina followed my gaze, grabbed my hand and pulled me into the Uber. I turned to look at him again as the car made its way towards the end of the street, through the thick of the traffic. His big, dark eyes were so full of sadness that I wanted to hurl myself out of the car as it began to pull away and throw my arms around his neck.

That's the exact moment I realised I was too late. I thought I could walk away. I thought there was still time to protect my fragile, little heart, to lock it away so he could never break it. I was wrong. He already had it.

I wonder where I'd be now if none of this had ever happened. Where would I be living? What would I be doing? Would I have found someone new to sit up all night drinking Jack and Diet Coke with and talking about the future?

It's strange to think that if I had done things differently, I could have spared myself the most agonising pain of my life. Perhaps I'd still have my job, my home, and my friends. If I could only go back and change things, I could cut out the worst year of my life. But if I did that, I'd have to cut out the best year of my life, too. And honestly, I don't think that would be a fair trade.

Deep down, I always knew the heartbreak was coming. The happily-ever-after I'd dreamed of for us was always too good to be true. There was no use fighting it anymore, though. I knew I couldn't stay away from him. From that night on, we were inseparable. And that's the story of how Fate finally knocked me out cold.

Chapter 4

People say it's human nature to glamorise the things we no longer have — that we look back on bygone memories with rose-tinted glasses and omit anything less than wonderful from our recollections. But I can honestly say that, during the entire first year of my relationship with Dylan, there was nothing unpleasant to omit. We were so sickeningly happy that I don't know how anyone could stand to be around us.

We were simply besotted with each other. As soon as we discarded the battered pretence of friendship, all of the feelings we'd been trying so hard to squash down inside of ourselves came bursting to the surface. That magnetic force that seemed so intent on pulling us together only grew stronger. It just felt right.

I woke up every morning and said a little prayer to God (or the Universe or the giant hamster wheel in the sky — whoever it is that's running this show) to say thank you. I felt like I'd finally found what I'd spent all those years searching for. I was finally content.

In fact, I was more than content. I was brimming over with happiness. I lived in a luxury apartment with my best friend; I had a boyfriend more kind, thoughtful, and loving than I'd ever thought possible; I spent my weekends on private beaches drinking champagne or sipping cocktails at pool parties. I was living a life beyond my wildest dreams. Sometimes all I could do was interlace my fingers in Dylan's, try to take it all in, and whisper to myself, "I can't believe this is my real life. It's so perfect."

Then came that awful evening, just a few months after we became a couple, when Dylan had to fly back to the US. I sat, tangled up in his arms, and cried as he kissed my forehead and promised me that everything would be fine.

"Is this really going to work?" I sobbed. "Are we just stupid to try to do long distance?"

"I love you," he told me. I felt his arms tighten around me as if he were truly terrified to let me go. "I'd rather be in a long-distance relationship with you than not at all." My tears dripped down onto his arms. "It won't be for long," he assured me.

His deep brown eyes were damp with sadness when he gave me a final kiss goodbye. Then he headed into the hot, sticky evening to get on a plane that would take him thousands of miles away. It hurts to have your heart dragged that far away from you.

But even during those long, painful months we spent apart, our relationship was strong. We spoke to each other on the phone at least twice a day, and sent thousands of text messages back and forth. We flew to the other side of the world to visit each other and meet each other's families.

The dream of a future together pulled us through the heartache and loneliness of it all. The distance didn't unravel us. In fact, it made us surer than ever that we were meant to be together. So, by the time Dylan flew back to Bahrain for his second deployment at the beginning of 2020, it was easy to slip back into our old little slice of perfection. Once again, I found myself filled to the brim with warmth and love, whispering, "I can't believe this is my real life."

I can't believe this is my life – that became my unofficial mantra.

It's what I told myself each time Dylan brought me a coffee on a Saturday morning and woke me up with a kiss. It's what I thought when I heard him say he was proud of me. It's what I whispered to myself that day we sat on my bed and told each other how desperately we loved each other for the first time. And it's what I shrieked in disbelief the day he asked me to marry him.

I had woken up that morning with the sun streaming in through a little gap between the curtains. Dylan was already awake, sitting up next to me and scrolling through his phone. He smiled over at me as I opened my eyes.

"Good morning, babe," he said.

"Good morning," I said.

I stared up at him in a way that probably would have seemed downright psychotic to someone who didn't know me better. I was just so full of love for this man that I felt like my heart would burst. I couldn't tear my gaze away from him. I was simply in awe of him and how fully and completely he had transformed my life. I wrapped myself up in his arms and wished I could stay like that forever. Or at least until the coffee was ready.

"One of the girls at work wants to go get a manicure this morning. Do you mind taking her to the place you go to?"

I scrunched up my nose. I don't enjoy questions in the morning. In fact, the only thing I do enjoy in the morning is large quantities of caffeine.

"I just went and got my toenails done last week," I said. "And I want to spend the morning with you."

"You can get your fingernails painted," he said. "My treat."

It was a weird suggestion. I hate getting my fingernails painted. The moment one of those things starts to chip, I don't know a moment of peace inside my head. It's not worth the upkeep. Besides, Dylan had been working gruelling shifts on the base, and I wanted to soak up every possible second with him during one of his rare days off.

"I don't want to go," I said stubbornly. "I can give her the name of the place. Or maybe I could go with her one day after work. This morning I want to hang out, just the two of us."

He rolled his eyes and kissed the top of my head.

"Fine," he said. "If you're absolutely sure, then I'll let her know."

"I am absolutely sure," I assured him, snuggling back down under the duvet.

After a few hours had passed and several cups of coffee had been consumed, I sat down next to Dylan in front of the camera I'd set up on my dressing table. We'd decided to film a video together for my YouTube channel. We'd already been together for over a year at this point, but he'd only flitted in and out of a few scenes in some of the vlogs I'd uploaded. This was going to be the first time we sat down as a couple and made a video together. I was giddy with excitement about it. For years, I'd shared all of the different areas of my life with my YouTube community, and now it was finally time to share the most important part of all.

We answered relationship questions from my subscribers, laughing as we reminisced. Dylan had to stop me – not once, but twice – to wipe the lipstick off my teeth. Other than that, I thought the whole thing had gone well. Then, just as we were wrapping up the video, Dylan interjected unexpectedly.

"Actually, I have a surprise for Aimée that she knows nothing about," he said.

I looked over at him, confused. The only thing I could think was that he must have gone out and bought that new Xbox he'd been talking about for the last few weeks, though I had no idea why he'd want to share that news on YouTube.

He told me to close my eyes. I heard some shuffling and the creaking of my bedroom door. Then I felt Dylan's huge, rough hands on mine as he gently pulled me to my feet.

"Don't let me walk into the door," I said nervously as he guided me out of the room and into the hallway. It was difficult to tell if I was just disoriented or if I could hear another set of footsteps shuffling along the hallway with us. Slowly, he led me into the living room.

I opened my eyes and he squeezed my tiny hands in his huge ones. I instinctively looked over to where Nina was standing on the other side of the room, holding the camera. I turned my gaze back to Dylan and stared at him, wide-eyed, trying to calm all the hubbub that was going on in my mind. I practically felt all the blood rush out of my head, leaving my brain floundering in helpless confusion. I have absolutely no idea what he said to me. My brain exited the apartment complex. In fact, I'm not even sure it was still in the general Juffair area anymore. I couldn't hear the words he was saying. All I could hear was a voice screaming in my head.

He's going to propose. I'm being proposed to!

Don't be stupid. He's not proposing. Stop crying! Don't make a fool of yourself.

I felt my wide, confused eyes welling up. I tried to blink all of the emotion away before I made a complete fool out of myself.

What if he is? What if he wants to marry me?

I watched as he reached over and picked up a small box from the dining-room table. Then he got down on one knee and smiled up at me. My face was frozen into what I can only imagine was a particularly unattractive expression of utter shock.

"Yes!" I screamed at a pitch only dogs could hear.

Then …

Oh my God! I must be dreaming. I can't feel my legs. That means this is a dream. I'm asleep!

Dylan slipped the ring onto my finger. My hands were completely numb by this point, which only made me even more convinced that this was all an elaborate dream.

"Is this real life?" I asked as he threw his arms around me. "Because I can't believe this is my real life. I can't believe this is my real life!"

I stared down at the diamond on my finger, and a fresh wave of disbelief slapped me across the face. He'd designed it especially for me, himself – a gorgeous square-cut diamond in a band that sparkled so brightly, it looked as though it were made of magic. It was perfect. He was perfect. And I was a jabbering mess who still couldn't decide whether or not she was conscious.

"I can't believe this is my life," I said again, laughing and crying simultaneously.

"Yes, it's real life, babe. We're going to get married."

"Now I wish I'd got my nails done like you told me to."

It all seemed incredibly perfect. Somehow, in the midst of this crazy game we call life, I'd stumbled on a man who filled me with more joy than I'd ever dreamed of. He was kind and sweet; he brought me flowers just because; he held me close as we watched Disney movies in our PJs; he was everything I'd ever wanted, but never thought possible. And not only had I found this man, but he loved me and wanted to spend every day of the rest of his life with me.

I soaked in every second of this man's love. He made me feel safe. He made me believe I was worth loving. He made me feel complete. All of those feelings of inadequacy and self-doubt that had been weighing me down seemed to have melted away. In the safety of Dylan's love for me, I felt more confident and secure than I ever had. Surely that missing piece that I'd been searching for was this incredible person who made me feel whole. He was what I'd been looking for.

That life we were just starting to create together was so filled with laughter and happiness. We'd stay up late, drinking whiskey and dancing to George Strait songs. We'd get up on Saturday mornings and while away the hours at our favourite breakfast place. Even the most mundane moments seemed exciting when we were together.

When I went to stay with him in California, we'd go to Disneyland and run around like teenagers, soaking up the magic of being with the perfect person. It became "our place" where we could go and add an extra shot of wonder to our already wonderful life. Each time we'd walk into the park, I'd look up at the fairytale castle and think, *Cinderella's got nothing on me right now.*

We took dozens of pictures there, freezing some of the happiest moments of my life into snapshots of us living our own little fairytale. He posted those pictures of us on Instagram, smiling in our Disney bubble with the caption: *Such an amazing day #takemeback.*

I don't look back at that time with rose-tinted glasses. I remember it as being the happiest, most love-filled time anyone could ever hope for because that's exactly what it was. I loved my job, my friends, my apartment, and the feeling of waking up each day and knowing I was finally complete. It was a magical time with no hidden bitterness or worries.

But that magic wasn't meant to last. This wasn't my fairytale ending and, as impossible as it might have seemed back then, Dylan and I weren't destined to live happily-ever-after together. Just as quickly as all of that magic flooded into my life, it vanished again and left me reeling in the wake of it all.

Chapter 5

Bahrain had gone into lockdown three days before Dylan and I got engaged, which is why (he later told me) we got engaged barefoot in my living room. At first, the threat of the Covid-19 pandemic had just nipped at the edges of our little Bahrain bubble. We were assured that there was no need to worry – there weren't any cases on the island. The schools were closed as a precautionary measure for two weeks. But then that two-week closure got dragged out for another two weeks, and then another.

The bridge that snaked across the water to Saudi Arabia was closed, and Nick told me that the airports would quickly follow suit. Even amid all of the upheaval and uncertainty, we still felt safe during those first few weeks. We still went out for brunch on the weekends, and Nina and I would slip off to the beach as soon as our online lessons were finished. Our lives continued as normal with nothing but a vague sense of potential danger lurking in the background. Covid was rampaging from one country to the next, but we felt untouchable on our little island in the Persian Gulf.

But we weren't.

On St Patrick's Day of 2022, everyone in Bahrain received a text message stating that, as of midnight, the entire country would be locked down indefinitely. Nina burst into my room with her phone in her hand.

"Did you see it?" She let out a short, nervous laugh. "They're closing everything."

"I know," I said, already itching with a strange sense of claustrophobia. "I'm worried. There are only three cases here now, but what if it spreads? Does our health insurance cover this? Are we ever going to be able to fly home? What if people see this message, completely freak out, and start looting and rioting in the streets?"

"Aims, I think that may be a little dramatic ..."

"It could be like a dystopian novel!" I insisted, pacing back and forth in front of her and flapping my hands around nervously. My fear was already spiralling out of control, dozens of potential realities whirling through my brain.

"Stop!" Nina said. She grabbed me by the shoulders and looked me square in my wide, distressed eyes. "We're going to be fine. This is going to be okay."

I nodded and took a few deep breaths.

"Anyway," Nina added with a shrug, "it will all be over before Ramadan."

It wasn't over by Ramadan.

The temporary lockdown dragged on from weeks to months and the long, stifling days that had seemed so idyllic when we were sitting next to the pool or sipping cocktails in an air-conditioned bar started to become unbearable. All of the communal areas in our apartment complex had been cordoned off except for the running track that looped around the two tall, silver towers, exposed to the full glare of the sun. Nina and I tried to make the most of this small outdoor space once and then abandoned the idea. It was already above 40 degrees Celsius most days and even the evening air was thick and sticky. So we locked ourselves up in the apartment instead.

At first, we had made the best of a bad situation and found ways to keep ourselves entertained. We painted, did workout videos, watched movies, and attempted (and mostly failed at) preparing new recipes. One afternoon, we tore open a box of White Claws, threw on our high heels, and danced around the living room for a few hours, trying to pretend we'd escaped those same four, white walls for a while. Like most other people at that time, we were starting to feel the effects of cabin fever. The languid days stretched out, melting from one to another in a series of long, repetitive hours that had no end in sight.

Dylan went out to work as usual because repairing boat engines for the navy wasn't something he could do over Microsoft Teams in his PJs. He saw other rooms and spoke to other people. He could sit down in the cafeteria and order lunch from a menu. He would walk into the apartment after a full day of work and wonder why I hadn't been able to peel myself off the sofa. He didn't understand why I was so desperate to drag out the weekly trip to the supermarket. He was baffled by my frustrated tears. In response, I found myself feeling resentful towards him. I envied the fact that he woke up every morning and could leave. He had somewhere to go, something to do, while I rattled around the apartment, losing all sense of time and purpose.

Lockdown undoubtedly put stress on our relationship, but even before the effects of the stay-at-home orders had started to take hold, things had begun to shift, unexpectedly and uncomfortably, within our relationship. Until the day we got engaged, we'd never fought. There had never been a raised voice or an angry word between us. The closest we'd ever got to an argument was on the nights we'd lie in bed and I'd try to put my freezing feet on his legs to warm them up.

"Babe, I love you, but no!" he'd say, shifting further away from me.

"But my feet are so cold," I'd whine.

"Go and put some socks on then."

"What's the point of having a boyfriend if you have to wear socks to bed?" I'd asked grumpily, rolling over to grab a pair of socks from the bedside dresser.

That was it. That was the full extent of our disagreements. There was just no reason for us to argue. We agreed on practically everything, and the things we didn't agree on were so small and insignificant that they weren't worth getting upset about. Sure, Dylan might not want to order Dominos one night, but it was hardly worth starting an argument over.

After the proposal, things changed.

Of course, we basked in pre-marital bliss for a while. My heart had been full to the brim with love for him before, but now that we were getting married, it seemed to expand to the point of practically bursting open. The hours we whiled away talking about the future took the edge off the chaos that was mounting in the virus-rattled outside world. We looked forward to a life after lockdown, after Bahrain, after the wedding and the house-buying, when we would simply be husband and wife.

"I'm going to be Mrs Stevenson," I said, smiling up at Dylan one afternoon. No matter how many times I said it, I could never quite believe it.

"Yes, you are. You're going to be my wife!" He pulled an expression of mock terror. I laughed as he reached down and grabbed my hand, twirling my engagement ring around my finger. The diamond sparkled in the afternoon sun.

"Then you have to make a promise," I said.

"What kind of promise?"

"You have to tell me you love me every single day for the rest of my life." I smiled as I said it, but I was serious. For some reason, I suddenly needed this assurance from him. I had to know that I could always depend on his love for me.

"Now that is definitely something I can do." Dylan smiled and raised my hand to his lips. "I promise that, no matter what, I will tell you that I love you, every single day."

"Even if you're angry at me?"

"When am I ever angry at you?" He laughed.

"Maybe one day I'll really annoy you," I said. "But you still have to tell me you love me, okay?"

"I promise."

The problem was, that future we had dreamed of was hurtling towards us for real. We were planning a wedding and looking for condos. We needed concrete plans, and to start making huge commitments. It was only then that I realised that all the plans we'd been making together until that point weren't as solid as I'd believed they were. I thought we'd be able to reach up, pluck them out of the sky, and turn them into our reality. But when I tried to grab them, my fingers closed around empty wisps of dreams that turned out to be purely ornamental. They had no substance. They were never meant to come true.

Our plans had never been too intricate, but they'd been consistent. My teaching contract in Bahrain would end in June, and Dylan's deployment would end in September. We decided it would be best for me to go back home for the summer to spend some time with my family, partly because the Covid cases in Bahrain were already steadily rising to worrying levels, and partly so my mother could help me pick out my wedding dress.

We decided that we would get married in Italy. It was always going to be a logistical nightmare, trying to plan an event for a guest list that spans the entire globe. Dylan's family members were all back in the US, and mine were in the UK. Between us, we had friends spread over most of Asia and Europe. Whichever way we went about it, our wedding was going to be an inconvenience to someone, so we eventually decided we might as well make it an inconvenience to everyone and have it somewhere we'd always dreamed of visiting together.

After the wedding, we'd move to California, where I could begin the long and complicated process of applying for a Green Card. We'd buy a condo and make the most of every square inch of whatever California real estate we could afford. We'd visit Disneyland as often as possible because … Why wouldn't we? After a few years, when we were ready to start a family, we'd relocate to Scotland. Yes, it would be a struggle to leave behind that glorious west coast sunshine, but free healthcare, paid time off, and statutory maternity leave are all a lot more attractive when you have a growing family.

Things should have been perfect. It should have been the beginning of our fairytale forever. Instead, the perfection of our relationship started to shatter about a month after the engagement. Those plans we'd spent all this time making together – that I'd always thought were so firm and reliable – became brittle and started to fall to pieces.

First to go were the plans for the wedding.

Nina and I were huddled under a blanket on the sofa one evening, pouring over pictures of bridesmaid dresses and sipping on glasses of wine. Dylan emerged from the bedroom and his face looked strained. He stopped next to the coffee table and stood, fixing me with a serious expression as he told me that our wedding in Italy was suddenly out of the question.

"I just got off the phone with my dad. He said it's not right for me to ask my family to fly that far."

"It is a long way," I agreed, and threw an exasperated glance up at the ceiling to reproach the Universe for making things so difficult. "It's so annoying that everyone lives so far apart. But there's no option that's going to suit everyone. No matter what we do, people are going to have to travel. I think we should just go with the place that's going to make us happy."

"No," Dylan said firmly and shook his head. "I'm sorry, babe, but we're not getting married in Italy."

"I think I'm going to go Facetime my parents," Nina said quietly. She gathered up her stuff, and scurried into her bedroom and away from the awkward silence that had descended on the living room.

"If you don't want to get married in Italy, where are we going to have the wedding?" I asked.

"It's going to have to be in California," he said with a sigh.

Just like that, our plans for the wedding crumbled into dust and, after that, everything else seemed to fly up in the air too. Suddenly, changes seemed to be happening left, right and centre. One minute, we were looking at condos to buy in San Diego. Next, Dylan wanted to rent an apartment in San Jose. Briefly, the idea of Arizona popped up, seemingly out of nowhere. I watched helplessly as, every day, our future shapeshifted from one potential outcome to the next, never pausing for long enough to become anything tangible.

I didn't object to the spontaneity. After all, I'm the girl who packed her bags and jetted off to live in the Middle East on no more than a whim. I change my mind 50 times a day. Even right now, as I write this, I'm sitting in a hotel room in Italy that I booked out of the blue last night. I'm all for being spontaneous, and I understand that sometimes plans change. The problem was, I couldn't keep track of any of the changes that were happening because I wasn't involved in any of the decision-making. I felt overwhelmed, confused, and shut out. It was as if I were simply a bystander in my own life, watching my future rattle from one road to another, steered by someone else.

It wasn't that Dylan was intentionally trying to shut me out, and I don't think he ever intended to make me feel as if the rug had been yanked out from beneath my feet. It just became very apparent that I had pinned our future on the plans we'd talked over time and time again. I thought those plans *were the plan*. To Dylan, they were just hypothetical scenarios that he threw out because they sounded nice. In his mind, they had no substance. And the unnerving thing was that now we were having to build new plans from scratch, and I had no idea what he really wanted.

As the jumbled mess of Covid-confused days tumbled on and the end of my teaching contract grew closer, I began to panic. The idea of giving up my career and my financial independence had always seemed daunting, but, as I watched Dylan struggle to piece together his own plans for employment, I started to wonder if leaving my job was a huge mistake.

"I was thinking," I said one day, crawling up next to Dylan on the bed, "maybe I should stay here in Bahrain for another school year. I know neither of us wants to live apart again," I said quickly before he could interject. "But if I keep my job here, then we won't have to worry about money. It will give you more time to decide what you're going to do next."

"Babe, I already know what I'm going to do next." The tone of his voice was strained. I could tell he thought I was nagging him.

I tried to make my voice sound the least accusatory I could as I said, "But you keep changing your mind. It's a global pandemic, my love. People are fighting to hold onto their jobs right now. If I keep mine here, then it will just buy us a little more time. At least we'll know for sure that we'll have my income."

"I don't want us to be apart for another nine months," he said. He looked sad and scared, and my heart ached because I knew exactly how that felt. "Please."

"Okay," I said with a sad smile, and I never brought up the subject of me keeping my job again.

For a few days after that conversation, I wondered … and I worried. I still felt sad and uneasy about walking away from the job that I loved. I felt nervous that Dylan would never figure out what he wanted to do. Most of all, I felt worried because the future suddenly seemed so chaotic. Could I really give up everything I cared about – this entire life that I had made for myself – for a man whose plans and dreams and wishes were apparently a mystery to me?

Isn't that what a marriage is all about – having enough faith in the other person to trust their judgement?

As a stubbornly independent woman, that was an uncomfortable thought. This was the man I wanted to marry. I trusted him with my heart. Heck, I'd trust him with my life. Surely I could trust him with our plans for the future, even if they weren't necessarily what I wanted — even if he couldn't quite work out what they were yet.

I sat on my bed one afternoon while Dylan was at work, mulling over all of this. My thoughts were so clouded that picking through them was like wading through mud. I twisted a strand of hair around my finger and stared into space with glazed eyes. I decided it was time to squash all my concerns down into a deep, dark, empty corner at the back of my mind. I leaned into the discomfort of allowing myself to completely rely on someone else. I chose to believe that if Dylan said everything would work out, then it would.

I pulled out my phone and re-read the email from HR for the hundredth time. Typing out a brief response, I thanked them for the offer to renew my contract and let them know that I didn't plan to take it. I would be leaving Bahrain at the end of next month. Then I began the process of packing up the perfect life I'd created for myself in Bahrain to begin a new one with Dylan … whatever that would turn out to look like.

Chapter 6

That chaotic, Covid-tainted spring of 2020 gradually melted into summer. Bahrain remained locked down, and the once-bustling streets around our apartment building were eerily quiet. Nina and I had long since given up on our hopes of having one last hurrah at our favourite brunch spot before I left the country for good. Dylan and I abandoned any plans for an engagement party, which was probably for the best, since we both still winced in discomfort any time the unplannable wedding came up in conversation. Ever since Dylan had vetoed Italy, it had become an unbearable topic of conversation.

Those long, empty days locked up in the apartment seemed to stretch on into a hazy expanse, but at the same time, the date I was meant to be flying back to the U.K hurtled towards me at an alarming speed. I was desperate for a change of scenery, but I also couldn't bear the thought of leaving. I still couldn't quite bring myself to face up to the fact that, once I did, I wouldn't be coming back.

"You could come back," Nina suggested one afternoon.

We were sprawled over the sofas in the living room, midway through yet another Netflix marathon. Pillows and blankets were strewn across the room and a half-empty bowl of popcorn stood on the coffee table. The noise of the TV droned in the background. We'd given up on watching it hours ago, but the incessant flicker of light on the screen was strangely comforting.

"You could go home for the summer, just like you planned to, and then come here for a holiday. You're not planning on moving to California until October anyway. You could come back in September for a few weeks."

"I could, couldn't I?" I said slowly.

"Look, by then this virus will definitely be gone and everything will be open again. We can go to brunch and hang out at the beach and enjoy being in the outside world again." She grabbed a handful of stale popcorn from the bowl.

"I do miss the outside world," I said with a laugh. "And if I come in September, then I can start to help Dylan pack all his stuff up. It would be kind of perfect."

"Exactly!"

"I just feel so sad about leaving," I said with a sigh. "And maybe it wouldn't feel quite so difficult if we'd been able to make the most of my last few months here."

"We had so many plans!"

"It's going to be so strange not living with you next year," I told her and she nodded, sadly.

"What am I doing to do? What if I accidentally set fire to the kitchen?"

We both laughed, but it was tinged with sadness. We'd been roommates for three years. The idea of not having Nina in the next room was awful. It would be like moving away and leaving one of my limbs behind.

Time continued to stagger on, sometimes seeming unbearably slow-moving and others seeming to tumble by too quickly. Eventually or suddenly, the end of June came and it was time for Nina to fly back home for the summer to visit her parents. Like me, she was desperate to escape the stale air of our apartment and the still-empty streets of Juffair. But, unlike me, she'd be back again in August to begin another year of teaching and soaking up life in Bahrain. I still hadn't quite processed the fact that I wouldn't be.

The evening she left, we dithered awkwardly near the front door. Neither of us knew what to say. We said goodbye to each other every summer when the school year was over, but in the past, we'd always known exactly when we would see each other again.

"Have a safe flight," I said, trying to force back tears.

"Thanks. You, too."

She threw her arms around me and we squeezed each other tightly.

"It's going to be so weird without you here," she said.

"I know."

We unravelled ourselves from the hug and I held the door open as Nina manoeuvred her suitcases out into the hallway.

"Bye!" I called.

"I'll see you soon," she said and smiled back at me.

As the echo of her footsteps faded away in the corridor, I shut the heavy front door of our apartment and cried.

It felt surreal to watch Nina leave the apartment for the final time. In fact, the whole of 2020 until that point had felt surreal. These weighty, emotional moments seemed dreamlike and impossible amid all the chaos and confusion that was going on across the globe. It was as if someone had pulled the plug and let reality drain away, leaving us all blinking in confusion, unable to work out what was really happening.

After Nina left, the long days spent stuck in the apartment were even lonelier, but Dylan would come over straight from work in the evenings and immediately light up the remnants of the day. I'd physically jump each day when I heard the loud click of the door handle and would immediately burst into a smile when I saw his face. Even in the midst of the strain our relationship was under, we were still utterly in love. Nothing and no one in this world could make my heart flutter in my chest like the excitement of knowing Dylan was on his way home, and nothing filled me with more joy than being wrapped up in his arms.

"How did I manage all those years without knowing you?" he asked me one night. "I just can't imagine not having you in my life now."

I would look into those big, dark eyes and see the same intense, almost overwhelming amount of love that I felt for him reflected back at me. I was scared and I was stressed, but when I looked into those eyes, it didn't matter. All that mattered is that we were together and I would have given anything to stay, wrapped in his arms, locked away from the rest of the world, forever.

Unfortunately, I had to leave.

Dylan helped me pile all of my stuff into the back of the van. The sun had set hours before, but the evening was hot and sticky. The air was damp with humidity, and even the short walk from the apartment building to the carpark had made me sweaty. Dylan started the engine and the van filled with cool air. I sat back, watching out of the window as we drove out of Juffair and towards the airport.

The lights of the city flashed past as we drove. I kept my fingers firmly interlaced with Dylan's, but couldn't bring myself to look at him. I felt as though I would simply overflow with emotion if I did. I was downcast to be leaving Bahrain, but relieved to be heading home to see my family. I was excited to start a new chapter as Mrs Stevenson but heartbroken by the prospect of being separated from Dylan again, even if it was only for a summer. That doesn't even take into consideration the sheer panic that was building at the idea of flying during a global pandemic. It's a wonder my head didn't spontaneously combust with the pressure of all of those emotions!

"I'm going to miss you so much," I said, still looking out into the darkness of the evening. I tried to force the quiver out of my voice, but it didn't do any good. Tears started to spill down my face.

"I'm going to miss you too, babe," Dylan said. He picked up my hand and kissed my fingers gently.

"I just love you."

"I just love you, too."

The airport carpark was practically empty when we pulled up. I jumped down out of the truck and Dylan unloaded my cases. The hot evening air enveloped us, and we were sticky and flustered by the time we had wrangled all of my luggage and began moving it into the airport. There was almost no one else in sight on the pavement outside, but, when the automatic doors opened, we were met with the chaos inside.

Everything looked different. Huge parts of the building were cordoned off and there were large, makeshift fences plastered with Covid safety posters. There was a one-way system that wound its way towards the check-in area, which was hidden behind a large black partition. As soon as we walked through the doors, we were descended on by members of staff who bombarded us with questions and began ushering us in several different directions all at once.

"I'm not flying," I heard Dylan explain above the tangle of voices. "I'm just helping her with her luggage."

Hands began to prod me towards the check-in desk.

"Sir, if you're not flying then you can't be inside the airport."

"Yeah, I understand," I heard him stammer as someone tried to prod me forwards and away from him.

"Wait!" I said, snapping my head back to look at Dylan. He was being shooed back out of the doors as someone tried to pull my suitcases away from me.

Usually when we parted at the airport, it was with a long, reassuring hug and a barrage of "I love you"s, but that kind of thing doesn't fly during a pandemic. The crowd of people continued to shout over one another and try to separate us. Dylan took another step back towards the doors.

"No, wait! I need to say goodbye to you," I said frantically as the airport staff continued to flap around me. In the midst of the hubbub, Dylan leaned in and his lips quickly brushed against mine before he disappeared back behind the shabbily erected partitions at the entrance of the airport. "I'll call you, babe," he called over the voices.

I stood, eyes welling with tears as I stood up on my tip-toes and strained to watch him leave.

That was the last time I ever saw him.

PART TWO:
The Bubble Bursts

Chapter 7

The flight from Bahrain to Heathrow was eerily quiet. The rows of seats all around me sat empty, and there were only a handful of other people dotted around the huge cabin. As we took off into the night sky, I watched the island below grow smaller and smaller until it was nothing but a scatter of twinkling lights in the darkness.

"Excuse me," I said to a passing flight attendant. "Could I have a cup of coffee, please?"

"We can't serve coffee due to Covid-19 restrictions," she explained from behind her mask. "But we have Coke."

"Oh, could I just have some water, please?"

"No, I mean we can only serve Coke," she said and followed up my confused silence with, "It's a precaution we've put in place because of the pandemic."

"Right. I see," I said with a nod, not actually seeing at all. "A Coke will be great then. Thank you."

It was a long, uncomfortable flight. Every time I started to doze off into a watered-down version of sleep, I'd jump awake with an unsettling feeling in the pit of my stomach. I slid my window cover up and watched the vivid red of the sunrise creep across the huge expanse of sky. There was no hope of getting any sleep.

Then, when we finally landed and my dad caught me in his arms at arrivals, I felt a wave of relief. I was home. There was a sense of solidity in that. After weeks of uncertainty and never-ending hypotheticals, it felt like my feet were finally on solid ground.

As hard as it had been to peel myself away from Dylan for another stretch of long distance, and as deeply as I'd started to miss him from the moment he'd left the airport in Bahrain, it felt good to be home. After all those months spent cooped up in the apartment in Juffair, I was desperate for a change of scenery and a sense of space. Even my parents' three-bedroom semi-detached seemed like a mansion compared to the same two rooms I'd been wandering between since lockdown started. After a few days at home, I felt a sense of relief from the pressure of all of that confinement. I began to relax into the new feeling of freedom.

But, as the stress and tension caused by cabin fever melted away, all of my other worries had space to breathe and grow. From the dark recesses of my mind where I'd stashed it away, the problem of the wedding cried out, desperate for attention. Then all of my other concerns about my uncertain future with Dylan picked up the chorus, and my brain became full with the noise of unease.

When I spoke to Dylan on the phone, I tried, tentatively, to ask for updates about our future together. Conversations on the subject had become strained and difficult. He didn't like the fact that I always seemed to be nagging him. I didn't like the fact that he always seemed unable to give me a straight answer. Having spent our entire relationship in agreement with each other, we simply didn't have the tools to dismantle this problem together. We didn't even know where to begin.

One morning, my mother and I were watching *Say Yes to the Dress* in the living room. As I listened to one smiling bride after another talk about her upcoming wedding day with nothing but giddy excitement, I began to feel all of my stuffed-down emotions bubble to the surface. I snapped.

"My wedding is going to be a disaster!" I said, and burst into tears.

"What do you mean?" my mother asked, startled by my sudden explosion of emotion. She quickly turned off the TV and waited for me to catch my breath amid my sobs.

"I don't want to get married in California," I told her through my tears. "But it's not even California that's the problem. The real problem is that we can't come to a compromise. It's California or nothing at all. That just makes me wonder if this stupid California wedding means more to him than actually marrying me."

I wiped tears away from my eyes with the back of my sleeve. Then, between sobs, I went on to tell her about all of the other changes that Dylan had been making to our plans. I described how the original dream life we'd concocted together was now nothing but a tattered mess, and how I felt like I had no role in helping to create the new one. I just had to hold on tight and see where we were going to end up.

"I feel completely out of control of my own life," I said finally.

My mother looked at me sadly and sighed. "Marriage is hard," she said. "It requires a lot of compromises. Unfortunately, your relationship is going to require a lot more compromises than others."

Ain't that the truth?

"It doesn't feel like a compromise, though," I said, shaking my head. "It feels like I'm giving up everything."

"Well, that's because you are giving up a lot right now. And later on, when you move to Scotland, Dylan's going to have to give up a lot, too. If being with him is what you want most, then that's worth making sacrifices for. None of this other stuff – the wedding, the apartment, the job – matters as much as the person you're with."

I let all of that sink in and tried to sort through my thoughts. I'd be able to give up my apartment and my job and my whole life in Bahrain because Dylan mattered more than any of those things. I'd tossed aside the plans I'd had before I met him of moving to Thailand in my thirties and travelling around Southeast Asia. So why was it now so difficult to give up these last few things? Why was I trying so hard to hold onto the wedding we'd outlined, the home in San Diego we'd picked out, and the fantasy we'd been building together for the last year and a half?

If he can't compromise on those things, it's because I'm not what he wants most.

Ouch!

I'd been able to walk away from everything for Dylan because being with him meant more to me than any job, apartment, or country ever could. It had been a struggle, but I knew without a doubt that it was worth it. Watching him fight so hard to cling to his plans made me wonder if I was worth the same to him. And it was terrifying.

That night, I lay in bed, staring up and the ceiling. All of those thoughts continued to wash over me as the clock slowly swept around from midnight to two am and then four am. It felt like I was drowning. Was I just being ridiculous? Was I thinking too much into this?

What do I really want most?

I woke up the next morning after a fitful night of tossing and turning, and I knew what the answer was.

Dylan, obviously.

It was going to require a lifetime of compromises and sacrifices. We would have to find a way to work together as a team to build a brand-new life that we both wanted instead of dwelling on the old plans we'd had for ourselves. It would undoubtedly be challenging for us to scrap the old visions we'd had for our lives as single people, but getting married meant writing a new story, and that was exciting. Most importantly, when faced with the question of what I wanted most, the answer was undoubtedly Dylan and everything else melted into insignificance around him. Surely, when I explained that, he would tell me he felt that same way.

Unfortunately, I learned a few hours later that he had been asking himself the same question, and had come to a completely different conclusion.

He Facetimed me that morning, looking serious and somewhat defeated. His usually bright, cheerful eyes were dull and vacant. "I had a conversation with my dad last night," he told me almost as soon as I answered the phone.

I felt everything in my body go numb for a moment. "He doesn't want me to move to Scotland."

"What … Ever?" I almost choked on my own words. "But he knows that we won't be moving for years, right? It's not like we're planning on moving there tomorrow."

"He said he wants me to stay in the States. He hates the idea of us raising our kids so far away from him one day, and I couldn't leave, knowing he felt that way. I'd feel terrible."

"Didn't you explain to him that it's a better quality of life? Did you tell him about the paid time off? The maternity leave? The school system? Did you tell him how much more affordable it is for us to live there?"

"Yeah," he said.

"Did you tell him that we want to live there? My love, I'm sure he'll just want us to be happy …"

"But I can't be happy there knowing that he doesn't want me to go. And besides, think about all of the things I would have to give up if I moved to the UK."

"I know," I said, overwhelmed with frustration and desperation. "That's exactly how I feel about moving to California. But I'm doing it anyway because I want to be with you. I can give up all the other stuff because you're what I want most."

Eventually, he said, "Aimée, I just can't make a commitment like that to you."

My entire body went cold, as if all the blood had drained out of it. I instinctively glanced down at my engagement ring. Hadn't we already done the commitment thing? True, we hadn't officially mouthed the words "Til death do us part" yet, but it hadn't occurred to me that this whole time I'd been on some kind of matrimonial probationary period. Call me crazy, but he'd asked me to marry him and I'd said yes – I'd assumed that meant we were both on board to … you know … get married!

"But …" I whimpered, and realised I had nothing to say. There were no words I could use to convince him that I should be what he wanted most. Nothing I could say to him would make him decide that I was worth it. Clearly, I wasn't.

All at once, a thousand realisations came crashing down and smothered me. The pain in my chest was so intense, I could barely breathe. I had just given up everything. I had no job and no apartment. I'd packed my bags to move to the other side of the planet where I had no real desire to live, all because, when you really, truly love someone, you make those kinds of sacrifices. But I'd done all of that for someone who couldn't do the same for me. Had I really spent this whole time clinging so desperately to this man, praying so hard that he would never hurt me, that I'd been blind to the fact that I was holding it all together alone?

"I love you," I said finally and hopelessly.

"I love you, too, Aimée," he said. He pressed the heels of his hands into his eyes to stop the tears. "What are we going to do?" His face was strained with pain, and I would have given anything to reach out and touch him, to crawl into his arms, and breathe in the smell of him. I wanted to wipe away his tears and soothe away the pain. But, at the same time, I knew what he was really asking was, *What are you going to do?*

Was I prepared to make another sacrifice to shelter us both from the pain of losing each other? Could I continue to throw away the things I wanted for him now that I knew he would never be able to do the same for me? In that moment, I realised that what I really wanted most was a fairytale that could never come true.

"There's nothing we can do," I said, and waited, suspended in painful turmoil, for the answer I wanted but knew I wouldn't get.

Because, of course, I wanted him to shake his head and say, *No. I love you. I need to be with you, and I'm willing to do whatever I have to do to wake up next to you every day for the rest of my life like I promised I would.*

But that's not what he said. He said, "You're right."

No! I'm wrong! It doesn't have to be like this.

"I love you so much," he said. "But there's nothing we can do."

But there is something you can do! Just say you want to be with me, wherever that is! Tell me that I'm what you want most!

"Oh …" I said.

Oh God, no! Don't tell me I've given up everything for this man, poured every ounce of myself into loving him and now he's going to toss me aside.

"I love you, Aimée. I want to be with you," he said.

Then be with me! You can!

"I just can't hurt my family by leaving."

What about our family – the one we were going to have together?

"There's nothing I can do to change it," he said quietly.

That's not true. You just don't think it's worth doing. You don't think I'm worth it.

"So this is it," I choked out.

The feeling began to creep back into my body and the heat of the blood pounding through my veins was scaring. Until that moment I never knew that emotional pain could overflow into physical pain. My chest tightened and ached. The sharp, stabbing sensation of pins and needles clawed at my hands and fingers.

"Are you sure you want to end it?" he asked.

I threw my head into my hands and nodded, silently. It was a pointless question. I didn't want to end it. It was already ended. In fact, maybe it had never really begun. The truth was, we'd been in different relationships all along.

"I love you so much," I said as tears poured down my face.

"I love you, too," he said, rubbing his damp eyes and trying to keep his voice even. "I'm so sorry, Aimée."

I can't describe the pain I felt when that conversation ended, and I realised that my entire life had been ripped apart. The person I loved most in the world had exited my life and he'd torn my heart and soul to shreds as he left.

I sat in tatters at the top of the stairs and screamed.

I couldn't breathe.

I had a panic attack.

I thought I was going to die.

I didn't care.

And that was just the beginning.

Chapter 8

Heartbreak was far more devastating than I'd ever imagined. It was as if a hurricane had come tearing through my life, clawing at every part of me until I was left standing shocked and in tatters. It was nothing like they make it look in the movies. It's not all throwing chocolate boxes at the TV screen and eating ice cream out of the tub for a few days before miraculously bouncing back, stronger, fiercer, and more glamorous than ever. There's crippling self-doubt, sleepless nights spent shivering on the bathroom floor, and a lot of hyperventilating. Heartbreak really has the potential to crack you open to your core and leave all your vulnerabilities exposed to the elements. It's painful.

I'd experienced breakups in the past, of course. I'd shed a tear over those failed relationships and had sent my fair share of regretful drunken text messages. I'd been hurt by those feelings of loss, but this was different. My heart had been bruised before, but it had never been broken. This was the first time I'd ever willingly given the whole of my heart away to someone else in the desperate hope that they'd treasure it forever.

I can still remember the exact moment I decided to let my walls down with Dylan and leave my heart unguarded and vulnerable. It was a few weeks after he'd flown back to the US for work, and we were adjusting to our first bitter taste of a long-distance relationship. We'd exchanged hundreds, if not thousands, of texts in the few weeks since he'd left Bahrain and we'd spoken on the phone during every possible opportunity.

We'd only been "officially" together for a matter of months at that point, but we were already in so deep. I had fallen so madly in love with him that it made me dizzy. But, as much as I loved him, I still struggled to believe he truly loved me back. It had nothing to do with the way he treated me. He couldn't have treated me better. His whole being radiated with affection whenever he saw me. He spoke to me reassuringly and always made me his priority. Everything he did was wrapped up in love for me, but I still couldn't accept it. Each time I started to let myself sink into the feeling of being loved by him, those old, half-forgotten demons from years ago would jump into action and convince me it was too good to be true. After all, I was unloveable; I didn't deserve this kind of happiness. It couldn't be real. It was just another disaster waiting to happen.

That afternoon, we were exchanging text messages as I walked home from work. It was still early enough in the year to make the afternoon heat bearable, but I squinted in the sun as I made my way through the streets. Tall, shiny buildings rose up into the clear sky on either side of me. I darted from the shade of one to the next.

Dylan: *I love you so much, babe. I can't wait until we can just be together always.*

He's so sweet!

Wait, do you really think he means that? He's probably going to get bored of you eventually and toss you to one side.

If he didn't want to be with me, he would have broken up with me before he left. He says he loves me. I don't think he'd lie about that.

Trust me – sooner or later he's going to realise you're not worth the effort.

I looked up from my phone screen and crossed the road in the direction of my apartment building. A small motorised scooter rattled past me. I weighed up my options. I could continue to barricade my heart and keep Dylan at a distance, preparing myself all the while for the possibility that he could walk away from me at any moment. That would keep me safe. That would take the edge off the pain if he really did decide I wasn't worth the effort. The other option was to let my walls down and allow myself to believe this man when he told me he loved me and wanted to be with me forever. That would make me incredibly vulnerable, but, if I dived headfirst into love, maybe all those doubts would disappear. The question was, if I handed my heart over to Dylan, would he keep it safe?

I made my decision and in I dived.

Me: *I love you too. So much! And I can't wait to be with you always either.*

Had I really been so wrapped up in a fairytale that I'd willingly done that? Is that what love is – being so besotted with another human being that you give them every part of you and hope they won't tear you to shreds when all is said and done?

Unfortunately, my heart had been torn to shreds, and I was slowly but surely coming to the realisation that I had no idea how to fix it. The movies lie! There's no cheesy montage that takes place. You don't just try on a bunch of cute outfits, get a haircut, circle some job ads in the newspaper, and then – ta-da! – in the space of a cheesy two-minute pop song, you're suddenly thriving again. It's long and it's difficult and, in my case, it came with a whole array of not-so-fun side effects.

In the months following my breakup, I experienced:

- Insomnia
- Panic attacks
- Heart palpitations
- Breakouts that made me look like a Dalmatian
- Headaches
- Nausea
- An unsightly rash that covered my hands for weeks
- Hives (yes, hives!)
- Oh, and my eyelashes fell out.

But what was happening on the outside was nothing compared to what was happening inside my head.

You're not good enough. You were never good enough. That's why he's gone.

Oh my God! I willingly gave up my job during a global pandemic! What the hell am I going to do with my life now?

I'm an idiot. I'm an idiot. I'm an idiot.

Oh no! I turn 30 next year. I'm going to be 30, single, jobless, and living at home with my parents.

I never want to get out of bed again.

Wait! How much does it cost to freeze your eggs?

I am the biggest failure in the history of the world.

What is so wrong with me that not even my own fiancé thought I was worth sticking around for?

I told you so.

These and approximately 5,000 similar thoughts of fear, despair, and self-reproach whirled around in my mind, non-stop, for months. I'd lost the person I loved most in the world. Not only that, but I'd given up my job and my home in Bahrain. Then there was the future I'd envisioned with Dylan that had suddenly crumbled into dust. Past, present, and future – all wiped out in a matter of a few weeks. It felt as though my entire life had collapsed around me. I felt like a failure, and the weight of that embarrassment only added to the overall sense of emotional chaos.

I couldn't bring myself to tell any of my friends what had happened. I was too humiliated. Instead, I used the remainder of my quarantine period as an excuse to wrap myself up in a cocoon of blankets and hide away from the world. Even when I was allowed to go outside, I didn't emerge from the dreary den I'd created for myself. I just wanted to stay there, in the darkness, forever.

"Right," my mother said in a voice of forced cheerfulness. "We're going out today."

"No," I replied flatly from under the tangle of blankets.

The initial pain of the heartbreak – that relentless, clawing ache in my chest – had subsided. After almost two weeks of continuous sobbing throughout the nights, I had no energy left to cry anymore. I just lay there, exhausted and defeated. I didn't have the strength to feel the hurt anymore. I was just hollow.

"We're just going to pop to the shop," my mother said. "You need to leave the house. The fresh air will do you good."

"I can't leave the house," I said honestly. My panic attacks had become so frequent that I was scared to step foot outside the front door. How would I possibly keep it together in public? How could I maintain a facade of normality when I was falling apart at the seams?

"Aimée," my mother said firmly. "You have to leave the house today."

I unravelled myself from the pile of blankets and scraped my greasy hair back into a lank ponytail. I pulled on some shoes and followed my mother out to the car, reluctantly.

"We just need to pick up some bread," my mother said as a clicked my seatbelt into place. I took a deep breath.

It's just bread. You can do this!

When we got to the small corner shop, I pulled my mask up over my mouth. It went some way towards disguising my pale, gaunt face. My eyes flashed around the shop as I followed my mother through the door, scouring the little aisles for familiar faces. The coast was clear – I didn't recognise anyone.

I followed my mother through the narrow aisles stuffed with crisps, chocolates, and biscuits, and right over to the other end of the shop where the bread was. I dithered awkwardly behind her as she pawed through the different types of rolls on offer. I heard the door fly open and my eyes shot towards the other side of the room. I felt my heart plummet.

"We have to leave!" I hissed to my mother through my mask.

"What? Why?" she said, looking around.

"Look!"

I nodded in the direction of the door with eyes cloudy with terror. There, picking up a basket, was my friend Hayleigh's mother.

"I need to get out! I need to get out!"

As far as Hayleigh's mother was aware, I was still newly engaged and floating through life in a bubble of happiness. If she congratulated me on my engagement that had already been ripped to shreds, I was convinced that I would spontaneously combust among the loaves of freshly baked bread.

From above the low shelves of packaged food, I saw her turn her head in our direction. I dropped to the floor and pulled my mother down with me. I was hiding in the bread aisle of the local corner shop.

I can't believe this is my real life!

As discreetly as possible given the adrenaline that was whirling through my system, I pulled my mother back through the shop and out of the door without being spotted. The moment the door closed behind us and the cool air hit my face, I ripped off my mask in despair.

"This is so embarrassing!" I cried. "How am I going to explain this to people? I gave up everything and I have nothing to show for it. I'm 29 years old, single, and living in my parents' spare room. How did this happen to me? What am I going to do?"

When we got home, I wrapped myself back up in my blankets and hid myself away from the world again. I was convinced that I would never recover from what had happened. I was sure the maddening sense of loss would never ease, and that the great, crushing weight of sadness would never lift. I felt broken. I was lost in a thick, grey cloud of despair, and I couldn't see how I would ever find a way back out into the light.

Heartbreak is nothing like they make it look in the movies, and not just because their cutesy, surface-level depiction doesn't come close to reflecting the true emotional turmoil of it all. It's also because when you

105

watch a cheesy rom-com, you know with a reassuring certainty that the heroine is being swept through her sadness towards a guaranteed happy ending. In real life, when your heart is broken, there's just a vast expanse of uncertainty. There's no feel-good plot-line and no script to follow. It's easy to convince yourself that happiness will never re-enter the scene.

So I hid away from everyone and everything, and wished that I could simply skip to the end.

Chapter 9

Those first few weeks of heartache bled into a month and then two. I forced myself to go through the motions. I announced my failed relationship to friends I hadn't even had the chance to celebrate my engagement with. I dragged myself out of bed every morning with tear-stained eyes ringed with deep, purple circles. I ate. I left the house. I talked to people when I had to. I poured all of the energy I could muster into putting one foot in front of the other, but I had no idea which direction I was meant to head in. It was as if my entire life had been thrown up in the air and I was still waiting to see where it would land.

I briefly considered going back to Bahrain in an attempt to claw back some of what I had lost, but it became obvious that my old life was unsalvageable. After I told her about the breakup, Nina began taking quiet but deliberate steps away from our friendship. At first, I'd refused to believe it, even as her responses to my text messages and phone calls continued to become less and less enthusiastic, and more and more sparse. By the time I broached the idea of my returning to Bahrain, she'd decided that our friendship simply didn't belong in the new life she had made for herself after I'd left. She made it clear that I wouldn't fit in with her new group of friends, and eventually stopped replying to my messages altogether. I was never able to piece together how such a strong friendship could expire so quickly, or whether there was anything I could have done differently to sustain it. All I knew was that, just when I thought the shattered pieces of my broken heart couldn't endure any more hurt, this new loss launched me into a new, deeper wave of depression. I gave up on the idea of returning to Bahrain after that. It would never be the same there without the people I loved.

The future I'd dreamed of was shattered and there was no going back to the past. I would have to carve out a brand-new path for myself instead. The problem was, that I had no idea where to start.

Thankfully, I had a little bit of help from the Universe.

I rolled over in bed one morning and reached over to my bedside table, fumbling for my phone. My eyelids were heavy from another night of disturbed sleep, haunted by nightmares.

That night, I'd dreamt that I was locked in an old, battered car that was speeding along the road with broken brakes. It ploughed onto a beach and through throngs of people who were laughing and partying on the sand. I screamed helplessly and yanked at the handbrake, but it wouldn't stop. It went careering off the pier and into the ocean. I slammed my fists into the windows helplessly and screamed to the people on the shore to help as the car slowly began to sink. The crowd looked down at me as more and more water poured into the car. Then Dylan emerged from the crowd and told everyone not to worry – I didn't matter.

Similar and equally horrifying storylines played on repeat through the few hours of sleep I managed to rack up each night. I truly was a psychoanalyst's dream at that point.

I yanked the duvet up under my chin and began scrolling mindlessly through my phone. For no reason in particular, I opened the Facebook app for the first time in weeks. There wasn't anything on there that I wanted to see. In fact, I'd been purposely avoiding it. One more engagement announcement from some half-forgotten classmate from 15 years ago might have pushed me over the edge. But, before I even started scrolling, the first post on my feed caught my attention.

It had been posted on a bloggers' page I was a member of, but almost never visited. A life coach named Sophie was looking for bloggers who would write a review of her services in exchange for three free coaching sessions. I felt an immediate pang of excitement. Then I saw the comments section. The post already had hundreds of comments from bloggers across the country. I sniffed, feeling disappointed. Even if she did think my blog was worth collaborating with, she'd probably never even see my response to her post amid that sea of comments.

Well, what have you got to lose?

I sent off my response and, to my amazement, I got a message back from Sophie a couple of days later. She explained that she was drawing up a shortlist of potential bloggers to work with and she wanted to arrange a Facetime call to see if I would be a good fit. A few days later, I sat down at the dining-room table with my laptop to talk to her.

The screen lit up and the room filled with the annoyingly cheerful sound of my ringtone. I accepted the call and smiled nervously into the camera. Sophie smiled back from her end where she was sitting against a pretty backdrop of bookcases. Her blonde hair was tied back into a neat ponytail and she had an assortment of papers organised in front of her. We introduced ourselves, and Sophie began explaining her process.

"I'm looking for people who have some problems or sticking points that they need help with. I've had a lot of responses, but I'm trying to narrow it down to just five or six people. Ideally, I'd like to find people who would really benefit from one-to-one coaching – people who have something they feel like they can't really work through alone."

I nodded with a nervous smile and took a sip of my coffee.

"Is there anything going on in your life right now that you think you may need some help with?" Sophie asked. She picked up a pen and waited expectantly for my answer.

"Actually, yes. A couple of months ago, my engagement ended," I started, hesitantly. Everything was still so raw that talking about it felt like jabbing at an unhealed wound with a pointy stick.

"I'm sorry to hear that. That's a hard thing to go through," she said kindly.

"Yeah, it has been really hard actually. I think it's worse because I was living overseas, but I gave up my job to go get married because my fiancé wanted to move to California. Then, when we broke up, I had to move back in with my parents because I had nowhere else to go. I can't find a new job because of the pandemic. I also can't leave the country because of lockdown. I'm just kind of trapped here, and I've lost my entire sense of self because it feels like I lost everything all in one go and I have no idea what I'm supposed to do with my life now. I haven't slept in months because I keep having these recurring nightmares that my ex is trying to murder me and …" I punctuated my shaking, rambling speech with a deep breath. I tried and failed to swallow back the sob that was preparing to burst out of my throat. "I can't stop crying."

There was a brief moment of silence as Sophie absorbed all of that information.

"Aimée," she said slowly, closing her notebook and putting her pen to the side, "I think you would really benefit from some coaching."

Sophie was right – I did benefit from coaching. Before our first session together, she told me to draw a picture of my life. In the middle of the page, I drew a sad-looking figure that represented me, totally enveloped in a dark, grey cloud and surrounded by swarms of question marks that hovered above my head. Off to one side, I drew a tall signpost with all of the arrows snapped off, leaving jagged edges in the wood and making the destinations impossible to decipher. Bulging, judgmental eyes glared down at me from the top corner. On the other side, I drew Dylan, smiling in his usual check shirt and baseball cap.

"It's a bit bleak, isn't it?" I said self-consciously as Sophie surveyed this chaotic insight into my mind.

"I think it gives a really good sense of how you feel," she said. "Can you explain all the different parts to me?"

"Well, that's me in the middle," I said, holding the drawing up to the webcam. "And I'm trapped in this enormous fog. It's dark and it's miserable, and I can't find my way out. I'm just completely lost in the darkness."

"Right," Sophie prompted me.

I suddenly realised how crazy this all sounded now that I was saying it out loud, but I carried on.

"Then this," I said, pointing to the broken signpost, "represents the fact that I have no idea where I'm going. All of the roads I thought I would go down are suddenly blocked off to me. The question marks are there because I feel plagued with hundreds of different questions and what-ifs at the moment. And then eyes are all looking at me, judging me. Everyone is looking at me, thinking I'm a complete failure."

"And is that your ex?" Sophie asked, pointing to the smiling figure in the hat. I sighed.

"Yes."

"Why does he look so happy?"

"Because his life kept going after the breakup. He moved back to California, just like he wanted. He got the job he wanted. He found a place to live. He was able to just keep going along the path he'd chosen for himself. I don't even have a path anymore."

"Not yet," Sophie said with a small smile. "But we can build you a new one."

I struggled through that first session. Sophie was patient and tactful, asking just the right questions to learn about my situation without forcing me to dive too deeply into my pain. I still couldn't help feeling guarded and uncomfortable, though. My words came out reluctantly. It was difficult, after having my heart broken so brutally, to hold up the remnants for a stranger to examine.

"I have an idea," Sophie said at the end of the session. "I want you to try a writing exercise. Writing comes naturally to you, and you may find it easier to express yourself on paper than you do speaking face to face. I want you to write a letter to him. Fill it with all of your feelings and all of the things you wish you could say to him. Be completely honest. Let it all out!"

"Okay," I said, already itching to grab my notebook.

"But whatever you do," Sophie added hurriedly, "don't send it!"

So I wrote. I threw my notebook open on the dining-room table and let all of the ideas that were bouncing around in my head explode onto the page. I filled that letter with all the hurt and anger that was weighing down my heart. I stuffed it full of love and affection, regret, and sadness. I wrote about our lost future, and demanded answers to all of the questions that had been tormenting me. I filled pages with memories and conversations we'd had, begging him to explain how he had been able to discard it all so easily. I poured everything into those crumpled pages from my notebook.

And, as I wrote, I felt the tangled mess of emotions in my head begin to unravel ever so slightly. The dark cloud I'd been trapped in began to thin. With every word that flowed out of my head, through the nib of my pen and out onto the paper, I felt a little lighter.

By the time I was finished, the letter was 16 pages long and stained with tears. I stared down at the messy wad of papers where all of the thoughts which had been trapped inside my head now found a new home. Then, just for a moment, I felt a fleeting sense of relief.

Chapter 10

Even with Sophie's help, moving on felt like a constant uphill battle. This was partly because sadness can feel like quicksand – sucking you under and making each step feel almost impossible – and partly because I still had no idea where I was moving on to. The world was still engulfed by the pandemic, which made future plans even more slippery and difficult to stack into place. That grey cloud I felt engulfed by had started the thin, but I still couldn't make out where I was heading.

So I tried not to worry about where I was going or what the heck I was going to do next. Instead, I focussed on trying to find myself amid the debris. After all, before I could even begin to think of rebuilding my life, I had to rebuild myself.

By that point, I had lost all sense of who I was. It wasn't just that I didn't recognise myself in the pale, dull-eyed reflection that stared back at me out of the mirror. My whole identity had unravelled, and I had no idea who I even was anymore.

Think about all of the ways you define yourself: job title; relationship status; friendships; where you live; what you do in your spare time. Now imagine waking up one day and realising that all of those things have suddenly vanished. Who is left standing when all of that is stripped away?

It was difficult to believe that such a short while ago I had felt so sure of myself. I knew who I was. Every part of my life had seemed solid; my future had seemed so certain.

My name is Aimée. I'm a primary school teacher in Bahrain. I'm engaged to a US serviceman named Dylan and we're going to get married and live happily-ever-after.

Who the hell am I now?

I felt so broken and so lost that I couldn't see how I would ever recover. I scratched around in the remnants of who I used to be, hoping I could resurrect her somehow, but it was useless. I didn't even know where to start.

"Start by doing more of the things that make you happy," Sophie told me during one of our sessions. More pages of frantically scribbled writing were sprawled out over the dining-room table in front of my laptop. Sophie looked out at me from the screen and I bit the end of my pencil uncomfortably as I listened to her. "You need to start feeling good again."

I didn't respond. The idea that I was even capable of feeling good again seemed ludicrous. I wasn't trying to feel good. Happiness wasn't the destination I was aiming for. I simply wanted to feel not horrible – and even that seemed painfully out of reach.

"It's not going to happen overnight," Sophie said as if she could tell what was going on behind my vacant stare. "But happiness is something you can work on. It's something you need to work on. That's what's going to help to pull you out of the cloud."

"I just don't know how to be happy anymore," I admitted. "I used to be so happy, I could barely believe it. I didn't even know it was possible to be that happy. Sometimes I would just stop what I was doing, look around, and say, 'I can't believe this is my real life!' It seemed too good to be true. And in the end, I suppose it was."

Sophie put down her pen and stared at me thoughtfully for a moment. "It must have felt really nice to feel that happy," she said.

"It did. It was overwhelming sometimes."

"Why was it overwhelming?"

"I don't know," I said with a shrug, trying to dig through the memories of that happiness for an answer. "I suppose because everything was so good. I felt so lucky. It almost made me wonder why."

"Didn't you feel like you deserved to be that happy?" Sophie asked.

I shifted my weight in my chair.

"Probably not," I said with a pang of realisation.

"Did that make it hard to really enjoy the happiness?"

I stopped and slipped back into the memories of my old life. I watched myself sipping cocktails with Nina, telling her that she was my non-romantic soulmate and that we'd be friends forever. I saw myself holding onto Dylan's hand at brunch, looking over at him every few minutes to soak in a fresh wave of joy at being with him. I heard myself say over and over again, "I can't believe this is my real life." It was as if someone had held all of these pictures up to a UV light that allowed me to see what had been lurking in the background the entire time.

"I was frantic," I said in disbelief. "I was obsessed with soaking up every single second of happiness … but not in a good way. I couldn't fully enjoy it because I was constantly so scared that it was all just going to disappear." I sat in the discomfort of that realisation for a few moments. "And then it did," I added finally.

119

"Sometimes we get so caught up in the idea of chasing happiness that we don't realise that it's far more important to be content," Sophie explained. "Happiness is like any other emotion – it comes and goes. Contentment is more stable. People always overlook it because it's not quite as glamorous." She smiled. "But we need to start by introducing small moments of happiness back into your life to lift you out of your grief. This week, I want you to do three things that make you feel happy."

"I can do that," I said with confidence.

When I sat down with my notebook to write out my list of three things later that afternoon, I realised that my confidence might have been slightly misplaced. I couldn't think of a single thing that would make me feel happy. I could think of plenty of things that would have made the old Aimée happy: cocktails at her favourite rooftop bar; an episode of *Say Yes to the Dress*; nachos from Big Tex BBQ and Waffle House in Juffair; a hug from Dylan – the list seemed almost endless. But I knew nothing about this new version of Aimée who walked around like a sleep-deprived pod person. What did she enjoy? What would make her happy?

Who the heck is she?

After what felt like an eternity, I scratched out my list.

- Watch a movie

- Drink a hot chocolate
- Go to a dance class

The first two were relatively easy to carry out. I could do both from the comfort of my living room from underneath my blankets, dressed in my unofficial uniform of pizza-stained pyjamas. I was surprised by how surreal it felt to do something that felt good, though. As I sat there, watching the Netflix movie, I could feel my entire body relax. Sophie was right: the sensation of happiness came and then went again, but I had felt it and that was pretty incredible.

The last item on my list seemed downright ridiculous. Lockdown measures had eased enough for socialisation to begin again, but I'd actively avoided it. My panic attacks were still so frequent that I tried to avoid leaving the house when I could and the idea of meeting new people seemed downright horrifying.

Why do I think this is going to make me happy?

I knew why. I loved the idea of dancing, but I'd always felt nauseatingly self-conscious about doing it in front of other people without at least half a bottle of wine sloshing around inside me. I had no concept of rhythm, and my arms and legs always seemed to jerk around erratically as if they weren't connected to the rest of my body. I'd find myself dithering at the edge of the dancefloor, wishing I could just let go and enjoy the music the way that Nina and Nick always had.

It was for this exact reason that Dylan had promised we'd get dance lessons before the wedding. He was just as likely to stumble over his own feet as I was. In fact, it's difficult to say which of us was the most rhythmically challenged. We agreed that we needed to get some practice in ahead of the wedding reception so we wouldn't be burdened with feelings of self-consciousness on what was meant to be the happiest day of our lives.

Well, I may never get the wedding, but I can still have the dance lessons.

I was terrified. As I made my way up the stairs towards the dance class, I felt nauseous with anxiety. Even before becoming a self-inflicted, blanket-wearing recluse, I'd been painfully nervous around new people. Now I was about to throw myself into a room full of strangers and dance in front of them. Why had this ever seemed like a good idea?

I pushed the door open slowly and peeked my head inside. Half a dozen other young women, all roughly my age, were already chatting inside the room. I gave them a shy smile, said a quiet hello, and scurried to the corner of the room to put down my bag.

I was painfully self-aware through the entire hour of that first dance lesson. I cringed each time I caught sight of myself in the huge, floor-length mirror, and was so self-conscious that I struggled to speak to the other girls in the class. But I enjoyed it! All of the nerve-wracking scenarios that had been swirling around in my head (tripping over my own feet in front of everyone, not knowing my right from my left, forgetting all of the moves) really did happen. I was a disaster. It suddenly didn't matter, though. Making those mistakes wasn't the huge, earth-shattering humiliation I'd built it up to be in my head. I was having too much fun to care how ridiculous I looked.

I went back the next week, and the next, and the next. For months, I cried all the way to the gym and all the way back, but for that one hour when I was dancing, I felt happy, immersed in my little world of eight counts. As time went on, that outer shell of awkward nervousness melted away, and that hour on a Wednesday afternoon became my favourite out of the entire week.

(It was on the drive home from one of these dance classes, many months after I'd first started, that I had a startling realisation. I was waiting at the traffic lights with my radio blaring and the window down. I was bopping along to the radio and singing my heart out. Suddenly, I stopped. I gasped. *When did I stop crying all the way home from dance class?* I flipped through the memories of my weekly trip to and from the gym, and realised that it had been weeks since I'd shed a single tear during the journey. This discovery struck me. By this time, the breakup with Dylan was becoming nothing more than a painful memory and I'd made incredible progress. Still, I thought back to all of those nights I'd sobbed myself to sleep and prayed for the day when the sadness would lift, and realised that I hadn't even noticed the change in myself happening. To this day, I still think forcing myself into that dance class on that very first Wednesday evening was a huge part of my healing process.)

With Sophie's advice, I started to piece myself back together. I discovered new hobbies and interests that I enjoyed. I continued to schedule time for happiness until, at last, it started to appear naturally throughout the day without a specific invitation.

I got a job at a college for students with special educational needs. It was vastly different from the job I'd had teaching at the fancy private school in Bahrain (so fancy, in fact, that two of the princes were in my homeroom class), but I immediately loved it. It helped to have something meaningful to wake up for in the morning and, while I was busy at work, there was no time for my mind to jump through its little puddles of sadness. I got on really well with my co-workers and, although I knew it was only a temporary position, I thrived with this new sense of purpose.

I was taking slow but steady steps forwards, and it felt great. Unfortunately, healing from heartbreak isn't linear. Instead, it takes you off in unnecessary directions and loops back around to places you've visited before. Some days, you can look around and wonder if you've made any progress at all. Then there are the times when you get snapped right back to the starting line.

I was committed to nurturing my mental health and becoming a strong, independent woman (circa Beyoncé 2001). The problem was, I was still a heartbroken fool.

Everyone knows that after a breakup you're not supposed to stay in contact with your ex! This, my friends, is a truth universally acknowledged. After all, how can you ever hope to build a new life without someone if that person is still in it? Immediately after the breakup, everything in me (and everyone around me) had told me the only thing I could do for what little was left of my self-respect (and sanity) was to go cold-turkey. I'd explained to Dylan that I couldn't talk to him – it was simply too painful and too complicated. I needed to focus on getting through this. Initially, he'd agreed.

But, before long, the messages started to drip through.

Dylan: *I don't want to upset you by texting you. I just miss you so much.*

After that came the drunken phone calls. "I just wish things were different. I hate this."

Then came the day he asked me, "Do you think we did enough?"

I felt my heart ache again. Fresh tears pricked my eyes.

"I did everything I could," I replied honestly.

Hello Sasha Fierce! Where did that little spike of sassy self-confidence come from?

"Yeah … I'm just wondering if I did."

No, you bloody well didn't! But you can still fix it. Just tell me that I'm what you want most. Tell me that I matter.

"I don't know. Maybe we just wanted different things," I said sadly and then almost choked when I realised what I'd said.

Why did I just say that? No! No, tell him you love him and you want to make it right!

"Yeah, maybe you're right," he agreed.

No! I'm not right. Don't listen to me!

There was a constant battle going on inside of me: Reason vs Romance. Reason showed up for life coaching sessions, pencil and notebook in hand, nodding with enthusiasm at all of the logical suggestions Sophie made. Reason got me up every morning and gave me the prod I needed to move forwards. Reason had started making a few vague, tentative plans for the future and, most importantly, Reason told me time and time again not to respond to Dylan's messages.

Romance, on the other hand, still had its claws firmly dug into the past and refused to let go. It had no interest in the future and could barely tolerate the present. Romance thrived each time a new message came through on my phone and eagerly encouraged me to reply. It whispered to me that things would work out after all, and that Dylan and I were destined to have our fairytale ending eventually.

With both Reason and Romance on the scene, I became stuck. I was trudging forwards with all the strength I had, trying to move on. But, by staying in contact with Dylan, I'd unknowingly allowed Romance to tie a giant elastic band around my waist, ready to snap me back to the starting point at any given second.

I still lit up every time I got a text from Dylan. I still said, "Don't worry. I love hearing from you," every time he apologised for not keeping his distance like I'd asked him to. I'd even started initiating conversations myself. It felt as though the same enormous, magnetic energy that had forced us together all that time ago in Bahrain was making it impossible, once again, for me to walk away. Something was pushing me back towards him.

Each time I heard a text come through on my phone, I still wondered, deep down, if this would be the message I was waiting for – the one where he told me he'd made a mistake and he needed me back in his life.

I never got that text. The message I got from him was completely different. And that message broke my heart all over again.

Chapter 11

As soon as Mark Drakeford, the First Minister of Wales, announced that we were allowed to travel outside of our home counties, I packed a case and drove up to North Wales to visit my friend, Gabby. Gabby is the kind of friend who will sit patiently and let you talk in circles about the same nonsense for an hour before giving very frank advice. It's rarely what I want to hear, but it's always right.

Gabby and I met when we were teenagers, in a shipping container in South Africa. That's not some kind of strange metaphor – we literally spent two weeks on the outskirts of a township near Johannesburg, where we slept in the same rusty, metal shipping container. We'd both signed up for a fortnight-long youth project where teenagers from all over the UK got together to build daycare centres and shower blocks for poverty-stricken communities in South Africa.

Unfortunately, the trip hadn't exactly panned out the way any of us had expected. Scandals, lies, and near-death experiences were not advertised in the brochure, but all came as part of the package. Apparently, there was some kind of underhandedness afoot with some of the event organisers that came to light shortly after we arrived. Whether we'd all been intentionally misled or it was simply a case of abysmal planning, safety and general organisation were practically non-existent that fortnight. We found ourselves camping out in some truly dangerous conditions, which was unnerving at times but helped to cement our friendship. After all, nothing will ever bond you with someone quite like living in a freezing cold shipping container with them and spending your evenings huddled in the dark, trying to untangle a web of potential fraud. At the end of those two weeks, I left South Africa with two things – pneumonia and a new best friend.

After over a year of lockdown and having my heart backed over by a rubbish truck, I needed a change of scenery and the comforting sight of a familiar face. I also needed Gabby's honest opinion. It had been a couple of weeks since I'd heard from Dylan, which was quite unusual, and I found myself aching with the absence of him again. I was done playing games. I was done with the cryptic messages we'd been exchanging this entire time.

Romance had finally triumphed over Reason by this point, and I was ready to make a bold (and completely ill-advised) declaration.

Something like:

I am still absolutely head over heels in love with you and, if you're worried that it's too late to fix it, don't be. It's not! I keep thinking about the conversation we had a few weeks ago and wishing I'd just told you then how much I still love you. Let's fix this bloody train wreck!

I pulled up in front of Gabby's cottage and stretched my stiff limbs. It was a long drive from my parents' house on the south coast all the way up towards the tip of the country where Gabby lived. I undid my seatbelt and sighed. I already knew what she would say about my desperate desire to somehow Pritt Stick my relationship back together. She'd tell me that Dylan and I lived on different continents. She'd remind me that he hadn't wanted to make compromises for me last time, and he wouldn't want to now either. She'd call me crazy. Then she'd give me a hug, push a glass of wine into my hand, and insist that I was too good for any man anyway.

I pulled my weekend bag out of the boot of my car and made my way up her drive.

"Hi!" she said, flinging the door open and wrapping her arms around me.

"It's so good to see you," I said.

Gabby led me inside with a huge grin on her face. Her blonde curls bounced around her shoulders as she helped me with my bags. Her dog, Chandler, leapt up on me excitedly, tail wagging and tongue lolling.

"Your house is amazing!" I said in awe.

Gabby screwed up her face, crinkling her nose. "There's so much left to do."

"But you have a house!"

As she led me through to the guest room, I marvelled at this new space that was just her own. Every inch of it reflected her personality unmistakably, from the pretty pink wallpaper to the Harry Potter memorabilia. She suddenly seemed like such a grown-up. Conversely, I suddenly felt like I'd tripped and fallen in a race and had stumbled back onto my feet to find everyone else was already 100 yards ahead of me. How could it be that all of my friends were buying houses and getting married, and I had to borrow my mother's car to make this weekend trip?

Gabby threw my bag onto the guest bed.

"So," she said, fixing her eyes on mine. "How are you doing?"

I decided to hold off on telling Gabby my plan vis-a-vis re-declaring my feelings for Dylan. I didn't want to spring it on her straight away, and I knew that it would be a conversation best broached over a glass of wine. Instead, I told her all about my sessions with Sophie and my new job, and asked her to fill me in on everything that had happened since the last time I'd seen her. I'd get her advice on Dylan later. There was plenty of time.

But, before I even got a chance to run the idea past Gabby (and then probably have it dismissed as evidence that I was certifiable), I got a text from him. Gabby and I had taken her dog out for a walk. We were meandering through the park, chatting and watching Chandler bound around after his ball. It was a fairly warm evening for early spring, and sunlight broke through the tree branches overhead. Gabby threw the ball again and Chandler raced after it, hurling himself into a puddle of muddy rainwater.

"Chandler!" she shouted after him. "Look at the state of you!"

I felt my phone vibrate in my pocket and a shiver of anticipation run through my entire body.

Maybe it's him!

Maybe the reason I hadn't heard from him was that he'd taken some time to mull everything over. Now perhaps he had finally come to the realisation that our relationship was something worth having. How weird would that be – him declaring he still loved me the day I was planning on declaring I still loved him? Nicholas Sparks couldn't write that kind of thing!

Dylan: *Hey! I know this might seem out of the blue, but I've started seeing someone else. I just wanted you to hear it from me before you see it online. I thought it would be better to tell you since we're friends. I hope everything is going well with you!*

"Oh my God!" I said, jaw hanging open. My despair echoed in the stillness of an otherwise lovely evening. I felt my body go numb, and worried that I might collapse into the nearest bush.

"What?" Gabby spun around with a worried look and walked over to me when she saw the way I was clutching my phone. I showed her the screen. My heart was pounding. I couldn't quite piece it together in my mind.

All this time I'd taken every text message and phone call, every time he told me he missed me, or called me beautiful to mean he still loved me. Heck, just a few weeks before he'd told me we should take a trip to Disney World together! Was it possible that all that time I'd simply been a stop-gap until he found someone better?

I felt devastated, angry, and, above all else, humiliated. I was embarrassed that my engagement had collapsed in on itself so easily, like a flimsy house of cards. I was embarrassed that the man I loved with an intensity similar to idiocy, had been able to replace me so quickly. But, most of all, I was embarrassed by how pitifully I still loved him, even then. All this time I had been falling asleep each night with a vision of him in my head while he'd been falling asleep in the arms of someone else.

"He's an idiot," Gabby told me, snatching the phone out of my hand.

No, I'm the idiot.

Gabby let me air my confusion of thoughts that evening. She listened patiently as I admitted that I'd secretly been hoping Dylan and I would get back together, and she kept my glass of wine topped up as I circled through the same unfathomable questions over and over again.

"I just can't imagine how I'm ever going to be happy again without him," I admitted.

"But you will be," Gabby said simply.

"It's just so unfair! I still love him. What if he really is my perfect person?"

"He's not your perfect person because if he were your perfect person, you'd still be together. Look, do I think he's an idiot for walking away from you? Of course! But his being able to walk away and find this new girl so quickly is the reason I know he's not your perfect person. Aims, your perfect person will stick with you, no matter what anybody else has to say. I know you love him, but if he really wanted to make it work, he would have."

"But why didn't he?" My eyes started to fill up with tears and I felt the familiar stab of inadequacy. Why wasn't I enough to convince him to stay?

Gabby pulled me in for a hug and I let my head rest on her shoulder.

"Would you like some chocolate cake?" she asked and I nodded.

I wiped my tears away as Gabby fetched us some cake slices from the kitchen.

"You're not allowed to reply to him, though," Gabby said firmly. She handed me my piece of cake and poured some more wine into my already-empty glass. "It's over and done. He's moved on. That message doesn't require a response. Just delete his number and try to move on too."

Suddenly, my phone screen lit up on the other end of the sofa. My eyes met Gabby's. I crawled over and picked up the phone. It was another message from Dylan.

Dylan: *Enjoy your evening, babe!*
Babe!

It felt like someone had punched through my chest and started clawing at my heart. I set down my glass of wine, worried that I might drop it … or launch it across the room in a fit of rage. All of a sudden, my mind went back to one afternoon in Bahrain. Dylan and I had been lounging at the edge of my bed, watching a cheesy movie.

"Have you called any of your other girlfriends 'babe'?" I'd asked.

He'd made an adorable *Oops … I've been caught out* face and I gasped, melodramatically.

"No!" I'd said with a laugh. "I don't want to be 'babe' if other people were 'babe'. I want to be special."

"You are special," he'd said, kissing my fingers. "Sure, I've called other girls 'babe', but you're the only one I've ever wanted to call 'Mrs Stevenson.'" I'd tried to keep up my facade of irritation, but a beaming smile broke through.

"I still think I need a new nickname," I'd said.

"No, you don't," he'd assured me. "You are that last girl I'll ever call 'babe'. You're the only one who matters."

Don't respond. Don't respond. Don't respond.

Me: *Please try to get the women in your life straight on your phone.*

Or go ahead and send a stupid response like that. That works too. I mean, I don't even know what that's supposed to mean, but cool.

Dylan: Aimée, *I'm so sorry. That wasn't meant for you.*

"What?" Gabby was shouting in the background. "What did he say?" I showed her my phone and she wrinkled up her face in irritation. "I can't believe he sent you that."

"I know!"

"And I can't believe you responded!" she said, wide-eyed. "I told you specifically, 'Do not respond to him!' A message like that shouldn't even be dignified with a response."

"I know," I repeated, feeling embarrassed this time. I flung my phone back over onto the other end of the sofa and tried to fling all of my emotions away with it. I felt hurt and defeated. Just when it had seemed like I had hit rock bottom, this new blow had sent me crashing through the floorboards and down into the basement.

I didn't sleep again that night, and I spent the next day feeling like an exposed nerve. My anxiety levels were through the roof and my brain was churning with a tangled mess of self-sabotaging thoughts. Why was this happening? How could I have been so stupid?

I dabbed concealer onto the deep, purple blotches under my eyes and took a deep breath. Gabby and I had planned to go to Liverpool that day so I could replace my battered, old phone and I was determined to enjoy it.

I did enjoy it. We both did. It was the very first day that pubs were allowed to reopen in England and, after queuing for nearly forty minutes, we got a table at a quaint beer garden a short walk away from the bustle of the city centre. Sprinkles of sunshine illuminated the new spring flowers and everyone was happy to be out and around other people. I suppose one of the strange side-effects of lockdown was that hundreds of thousands of people were united in their loneliness.

The final blow came when we got back to Gabby's house that evening. I connected my new phone to her Wi-Fi and opened Instagram to upload the picture I'd taken of us, sipping our drinks in the beer garden with wide grins. As I opened the app, I locked eyes on the first photo on my feed.

"Oh my God," I said again.

"What?" Gabby called from the kitchen.

"Oh my God!"

Gabby appeared in the doorway.

"Aimée," she said. "What is it?" The worry in her voice indicated that I must have looked like I was about to collapse. Heck, I felt like I was about to collapse!

"Is this …" I looked up at her and thrust the phone in her face. "Is this them at Disneyland?"

There it was, plastered all over my Instagram feed – the two of them cuddled up together, her smiling in her Minnie Mouse ears the way I used to when I was with him. And, below it, the caption: *Such an amazing day #takemeback*

Just like that, it was torn open – the wound I'd never allowed to heal. The one I'd been picking at for months each time I answered his phone calls or responded to his texts. Now I realised how ridiculous I'd been, clinging on so desperately to all the promises he'd made, to the faint glimmer of a chance that maybe he still felt the same way. For him, it was just a dream – a dream he'd woken up from and had already put out of his mind. For me, it was still a living nightmare.

I'd spent eight months patiently waiting for this man to realise he loved me enough to make compromises, that I was someone he couldn't live without. The reality was, he didn't. I wasn't. I could waste another eight months or even eight years of my life hoping for him to decide I was enough. But he never would. As much as I'd believed him (and I'm sure at some point he'd believed it himself) when he'd told me I was everything he'd always wanted, that wasn't true now. He was doing just fine without me.

At that moment, the heartbreak hit me all over again, even harder than it did the first time. The impossible dream I'd still been clinging to had burst like a bubble. Now it was time to wake up.

Chapter 12

I fell apart all over again after that trip to North Wales. If the breakup had shattered my heart, this new turn of events shattered my soul. It wasn't just the renewed sense of loss or even the sharp pang of rejection I felt when I realised how quickly Dylan had been able to move on. Those things were merely the catalysts that split me open and allowed over ten years' worth of repressed emotions and anxiety to spill out. And it was messy!

It had all unravelled – the patchwork pretence of "fine" that I'd been parading around in for the last decade. I'd convinced myself and everyone around me that I'd been able to walk away from that cruel, toxic relationship with Matt unscathed, but that wasn't true. I hadn't been able to simply dust away all of the feelings of self-doubt and inadequacy that he'd instilled in me. They'd been lurking deep down inside of me, festering for all of this time.

As I drove home from Gabby's, along the endless winding roads, I could feel it all bubbling to the surface: all the hurt; the feelings of inadequacy; every insecurity and self-loathing thought. I was overwhelmed with feeling them all at once so unexpectedly. It felt like I could crack open at any moment and they would all explode out of me, shrieking with maniacal laughter.

I suddenly realised why it had seemed utterly impossible to let go of Dylan. Yes, I had loved him. He'd been one of my most cherished friends as well as my fiancé. Of course, there was going to be a big, gaping hole left in my life where he had once been. But why had I been so resistant to move on and start filing that hole? Why did that seem like such an unthinkable undertaking?

I could see it now. Dylan had always been gentle and kind to me. He'd treated me with respect, and had gone out of his way time and time again to make me feel like I was important. He made me feel safe. He filled my life with so much love that it drowned out all of the hurt from the past. His compliments and words of love had mended the cracks within me that all of Matt's hurtful words had caused. Dylan's love had seemed so strong that I'd rebuilt my fragile sense of self on that foundation. When we were living in our blissful bubble in Bahrain, it was easy to believe that I was completely whole, content, and cured of all my past feelings of unworthiness. Now I could see that wasn't the case.

My self-esteem, my confidence, the belief that I was good enough – none of those things were ever truly mine. They were all just on loan from Dylan. Then, when he took back his love, all those other things disappeared, too. No wonder I hadn't been able to piece myself back together after the breakup. So many of the pieces were missing. Now this fresh news that Dylan had been able to replace me so easily just fuelled all of those old demons that told me I wasn't good enough and I didn't have a single shred of self-belief left to fight against them with.

All of these terrifying revelations hit me one after another on the seemingly endless drive back from Gabby's house. I sobbed huge, heaving sobs as my car sped along the winding country roads. Thick forests slipped past the windows so quickly that they looked blurred in my teary-eyed vision. It seemed as if my whole sense of reality were melting away around me.

"I can't see how I'm ever going to get past this," I told Sophie bleakly during our next session. After months of working hard to heave myself up out of the pit of despair, I'd collapsed back down to the bottom. I didn't have the energy to begin the climb again. I was exhausted.

I set my coffee mug down on the table in front of me. It had been three weeks since the unbearable drive home from Gabby's house and I was struggling. My nights were plagued with nightmares again and I was too nauseous with anxiety to eat. Weight had fallen off of my exhausted body and my eyes were ringed with purple like before.

"I feel terrible about myself," I said. "I just keep wondering what's wrong with me. Why was it so easy for him to forget about me and move on? What makes me so disposable to a man who was supposed to love me forever? Why am I not good enough?"

"Why did you and Dylan break up?" Sophie asked and her unexpected question shook me out of my reverie. She already knew the answer to that question. She was the poor soul who'd spent the last few months listening to me talk through that breakup on repeat. She waited for my answer expectantly.

"He changed his mind about where he wanted to live. He wanted us to live in California forever instead of moving to Edinburgh like we'd planned."

"But he wanted you to live in California with him," Sophie prompted.

"Yeah," I said slowly, trying to understand where she was going with this.

"So why didn't you?" she asked simply.

"Because," I spluttered, not quite sure how to answer. "Because that wasn't what we'd agreed on. He was asking me to give up everything, and he wasn't willing to give up anything at all. It didn't feel fair."

"But the option was there for you to go to California and marry Dylan and live there with him forever?" Her expression was unreadable. I nodded. "So you made a choice. You could have stayed with him if you'd wanted to. You could have ignored the fact that the relationship felt one-sided and moved to California to be with him.

"You didn't, though. You knew you wouldn't be happy in that life. Instead, you prioritised yourself. You walked away from the person you loved most, knowing full well how much that would hurt. You threw yourself into the unknown, even though you had no job and no house of your own to live in. You gave up everything because deep down you knew you couldn't be happy in a relationship with those kinds of dynamics."

I sat, stunned, letting Sophie's words sink in.

"None of this happened because you weren't good enough," Sophie continued. "This happened because you made the choice to make your happiness a priority, even when you knew it would be difficult. What kind of woman does that make you?"

I fidgeted uncomfortably. "I guess … a brave woman?"
"And?"
"And a strong woman?"

"Yeah!" Sophie said enthusiastically. "You're not a victim here. This isn't something that happened to you. This is a decision you made because you are a brave, strong woman, and you knew it was the right thing to do. It's awful and it's painful and anyone would be falling apart right now if they were going through the same thing. But," she added with a reassuring smile, "you did what was best for you. That's how I know you're going to be more than okay."

That concept astounded me. I had been so busy blaming myself, counting my inadequacies, and throwing myself the world's longest pity party, that the fact that I'd been the one who'd ultimately walked away had never sunk in. It did nothing to fill the enormous Dylan-sized hole I still had in my heart. It didn't make my future any less of a terrifying haze of uncertainty. But it gave me something to fight back against my insecurities with. Dylan and I hadn't broken up because I wasn't good enough. We'd broken up because it just wasn't the right fit. We wanted different things.

Somewhere, buried under all the heartache and tears, I'd already known that. We'd been drifting apart before I left Bahrain. As intensely as we'd loved each other, it hadn't been enough. We'd thrived in our little island bubble where everything dazzled in the sunlight. But, when it came to making our relationship last in the real world, we simply couldn't do it.

Love hadn't been enough to keep us together when the paths we'd wanted to walk down led to such vastly different destinations. But, instead of acknowledging that, something within me had forced me to believe that it was all my fault – that Dylan had discarded me because I wasn't worth keeping. I'd let all those beliefs from my past distort reality to fit their cruel narrative. It was all a figment of my tainted imagination.

Dylan hadn't left me because I wasn't good enough. We'd walked away from each other because that was the best decision for both of us. He'd found a new girlfriend and that was hurtful, but it didn't diminish any of the feelings he'd once had for me and, more importantly, it had absolutely no bearing on my worth.

PART THREE:
I Am
Enough

Chapter 13

Apparently, just having the *Aha!* moment isn't enough to change your entire life. You actually have to figure out what to do with that epiphany. I'd been optimistic (and downright clueless) enough to think that simply figuring out the root cause of the problem would more or less bring an end to this emotional dumpster fire I was experiencing. As if life were a game of Cluedo and, once I'd solved the mystery, I could throw the whole thing back into a box, forget about it, and get on with something else.

It didn't take long, however, to realise that simply knowing I needed to learn to love myself wasn't the end of the story – it was just the beginning. Now I actually had to, you know, learn to love myself. I had to undo a decade's worth of negative self-beliefs. If anything, facing up to all of my deep-rooted feelings of inadequacy and shame just set off a brand-new explosion of emotional upheaval. The demons that had been lurking in the dark corners of my mind for all of this time had been let loose. There was no hope of re-caging them, and I had no idea how to get rid of them. So, most Friday nights, I would try to drown them with wine. Needless to say, it wasn't a constructive solution, but I didn't know how to start working through all of the things I was feeling.

How does someone begin the task of learning to love themselves?

At any other time, I would have gone down the Eat, Pray, Love route and booked a flight to … anywhere! I wanted nothing more than to flit off to Italy to eat my weight in carbs and then wash up on a beach in Indonesia somewhere to drink cocktails and meditate until my heart magically mended itself. Unfortunately, we were still in the throes of a global pandemic, and leaving the country was not only a logistical nightmare but was actually considered a criminal offence.

It was as if the Universe had sat me down in time-out and said, finger wagging, *You're not running away from your problems this time, missy. You need to sit right here and deal with your issues, head-on.*

There was nowhere to run away to, no chance of distracting myself with a plane ticket like I'd tended to do in the past. Finally, I gave in and accepted the reality of the situation: I was going to have to go through my epic, life-defining, transformational self-love journey from the confines of my parents' spare room in rainy South Wales. It was hardly going to be the aesthetic post-breakup glow-up you see in the movies, but it was going to have to do.

Then there was that cumbersome question still looming over me, demanding an answer: Who the heck am I now?

Hi, I'm Aimée. I'm nearly 30, I work a zero-hour contract, and I live with my parents. I have no plans for the future, and my life is a hot mess.

It was a little bleak, sure, but at least it was a start.

One morning during this strange limbo stage, I woke up and felt like I was dying. Not from heartbreak this time. No, this time it was wine-related.

What have I done?

There were mascara-stained tissues scattered all over the floor. I had a vague recollection of sitting out in the garden, crying to the soundtrack from *The Greatest Showman* in the dark. My phone was propped up on the pillow next to me. My chest constricted with shame before I even unlocked the screen. I grabbed the phone, opened up my messages and, sure enough, there was a new conversation with Dylan.

Me: *I just need to be sure that you're safe and happy.*

What does that even mean? "Are you safe?" Note to self, Aimée: Be less of a walking bloody disaster, please.

Dylan: *Yeah, I'm safe. Thanks for asking.*

I wanted to crawl into a hole and die.

I waded through my shame and tried to think logically. Since returning from my trip to North Wales, I'd felt lost. It was as if I'd set up a comfy, little home for myself in Denial for the last eight months and, all of a sudden, I'd been evicted. Suddenly I had to face up to all of these difficult emotions and realisations and, instead, I'd chosen to give up. I was ducking and diving, doing whatever I could to try to outrun reality. But I couldn't spend the rest of my life drinking wine in my pyjamas and crying along to Hugh Jackman. This had to stop.

I propped myself up on one elbow and started writing a new message to Nick. He'd been stationed in Naples for the last few months and I'd been living my life vicariously through his photos of beautiful sunsets and pizza.

Me: *I drank a bottle of wine last night and drunk-texted Dylan.*

Nick: *Aimée! No! Man, you had a stroke of weakness.*

Me: *I'm asking you this because I'm actually still a little drunk from last night – do you think I'm going to be okay?*

I looked around at the disaster that was my bedroom. Last night's clothes were strewn over the floor and I'd knocked over a glass of water at some point. I sighed. It certainly didn't feel like I would ever find the strength to be okay again.

Nick: *Of course you will, Aimée. You're dealing with wild ass drama so of course it's normal to react this way. You're beautiful, smart, funny, and definitely fun so, in my eyes, you win at life. When you're able to, come here. We'll eat Napoli pizza and get white girl wasted together. After that, you'll have no more sadness in those bones.*

I sat up (with great difficulty because the room was still spinning) and planted my feet on the floor. I scraped my hair back into a frizzy ponytail and rubbed my puffy eyes.

This is it. You know that, don't you? If you don't make a change now … I'm worried.

I reached over and picked up my phone again. I pulled up last night's conversation with Dylan and began typing out a new message. A feeling of nausea gurgled within me, but whether that was because of the content of the message I was typing or the hangover was unclear.

Me: *I'm so sorry about last night. That must have been really annoying. The truth is, I've been struggling. I've spent the last eight months not wanting to move on or get over you because I really thought you were my person. I didn't think it was possible for us to stay apart when we loved each other so much. I've sat around this whole time, waiting for you to wake up one day and say, "I want to be with you!", and when that didn't happen, I fell apart. Now I'm ready to let go of all of that. I'm drawing a line in the sand and I promise you won't get any more weird drunk texts from me.*

That was it. I was done. It was time to move on for real this time, not just from Dylan, but from everything else that had happened in the past too.

An idea flashed through my mind. I went downstairs, grabbed a notebook off the bookshelf, and went out into the garden. Before I could begin the process of rebuilding myself, I had to face all of those old demons. I had to look them square in the eye. The best way I could think of to do that was by writing it all down. I could let all of those painful memories, limiting beliefs, and difficult feelings filter out of my head through my pen and out onto the page, just like I did with the writing exercises Sophie set for me.

I sat down at the table on the patio and started writing about the breakup. It was a blow-by-blow account of the worst day of my life. I recalled every word, every glance, and every wave of emotion I could, and scratched it all out in the notebook. Before long, my brain was churning out the memories faster than my hand could write them, so I pulled my laptop out and started typing instead.

I didn't stop for typos. I didn't look back to make sense of what I'd written. I just kept jabbing away at the keys, letting all those festering memories and emotions spill out of my mind and into the world where they seemed to collide with the fresh, bright air and instantly lose all their power over me. I wrote about all of the pain and the sadness, but also all of the love and happiness from the early days of the engagement. I let it all out and, with each stroke of the keys, I felt lighter.

Finally, I began to frantically type out the story of my relationship with Matt. For the first time in over a decade, I finally let myself acknowledge what he'd done to me. With each word I typed, I condemned the behaviour that I'd always tried to pretend wasn't that bad. Tears slid down onto the keyboard as I described the way that relationship had affected me. But I wasn't sad. I was relieved. Huge, knotted clusters of thoughts became untangled as I typed them out on the page, and it was surprisingly liberating.

The sun was starting to dip down below the trees at the bottom of the garden and the air was beginning to feel noticeably chillier by the time I stopped writing. My neck cracked loudly as I stretched and looked around me. I'd been absorbed in writing for hours. Then I looked back at the screen and felt a huge sense of accomplishment. I'd done it. I'd let everything that I'd been working so hard to push down finally come to the surface. And I didn't know it then, but I'd also written the first few chapters of what I had no idea would eventually become this book.

Chapter 14

As soon as it became public knowledge that my ex-fiancé had already snapped up a new girlfriend, my loved ones seemed to come to the conclusion en masse that I should start dating again, too. It felt like no time at all had elapsed between, "Congratulations on your engagement", to, "I'm so sorry to hear about the breakup", to, "So, you're still not seeing anyone new?"

I was less than enthusiastic about the prospect of hurling my heart at somebody new before I'd even finished duct taping it back together. Things seemed to be slotting back into place for me, slowly but surely, and I didn't want to rock the boat. I resisted offers of blind dates, stayed clear of online dating sites, and kept my eyes firmly on the ground any time I left the house, just in case (heaven forbid!) a man so much as made eye contact with me. I was boycotting men again and this time, so help me, I was sticking to it!

That lasted for approximately five weeks.

I swear I had absolutely no intention of dating again. In fact, the very idea of it made me feel uncomfortable. For that reason, I can't explain why I found myself downloading a new dating app on my phone one evening. I'd been sitting in my dressing gown with my hair piled on top of my head in a loose bun. I was mindlessly devouring one TikTok video after another and munching on a chocolate chip cookie. I scrolled up to see the next video and an advert appeared instead, flashing a variety of five-star reviews from now loved-up couples. I halted mid-scroll.

This could be a sign from the Universe that it's time to start dating again.

It could also just be very clever targeted advertising. Remember last week when a Facebook advert tried to sell you an online course called "How to finally keep that man"?

I stared down at my phone screen as the advert continued to loop, over and over again, and asked myself, *Am I really ready to start dating again?*

On the one hand, the idea of being with someone new made me uncomfortable to the point of nausea. I knew my relationship with Dylan was a thing of the past and there was no possibility of going back. I was finally okay with that. But, as ready as I was to create a new life without him, there was no denying that I was still in love with him.

It wasn't the all-consuming kind of love I'd felt when we were together, or even the soul-crushing love I'd felt when we broke up. There was just a trace of it left over, but it was enough to make me cringe at the thought of being with anyone else.

On the other hand, if Dylan could be happy prancing around with someone new so soon after the breakup, why couldn't I? If I really was ready to move on and leave the past behind me, shouldn't I start doing that sooner rather than later?

I wasn't convinced, but I pressed the "download" button anyway and began perusing the app. I felt beyond awkward. In spite of all of my friends' happily-ever-after Tinder stories, I still found the idea of online dating extremely uncomfortable. There was something strangely off-putting about scrolling through pictures of men and swiping left and right as if I were online shopping for a new pair of boots. To make matters worse, every single potential match I came across was lacking one vital element – they weren't Dylan.

And that's a good thing because Dylan isn't the right person for you.

In spite of my gut feeling that this whole thing was a truly horrible idea, I gritted my teeth and persisted with the swiping. Eventually, I matched with three men. One was incredibly boring and exclusively sent one-word messages; another was obsessed with talking about himself and what a wonderful catch he was; and the third, for all intents and purposes, was just right. The Goldilocks porridge of the dating world, if you will.

His name was James, and he was a trainee surgeon who loved to travel and spent his free time writing short stories. It was as if the Universe had looked down at me with pity and said, *Well, she's had a rough few months. Why don't I send over her perfect man as a little pick-me-up?*

I should have been thrilled. This cute, charming future doctor should have taken my mind off Dylan completely. Instead, I found myself squirming with indecision when he asked me out on a date.

"What is wrong with you?" my friend Taylor spluttered the next day at work. "You said he seems nice and you have lots in common. He's going to be a doctor! Why wouldn't you go out with him?"

"I don't know …" I murmured. She was right, after all. Some women spend their entire lives looking for Mr Right and, seemingly, mine had flashed up as a notification on my phone with minimal effort on my part. What was my problem?

"Let me see a picture of him," Taylor demanded. I handed over my phone and she collapsed into the chair next to me, eyes wide with disbelief. "He's gorgeous!" she exclaimed, flashing the phone screen at me. "God, if I were single, I'd be right in there. He's good-looking and smart and likes to travel and," she said, with emphasis. "Surgeons are rich!"

"I just don't know if I'm ready to date," I told her. She continued swiping through James's photos, pausing only to shoot me another look of disbelief. "It just feels weird."

"I say this as your friend," Taylor said, handing back my phone and looking me square in the eye. "You seriously need to get laid."

I agreed to go on the date – not because I had any intention of getting laid, but because the idea of dating struck such feelings of terror and revulsion in me that I was starting to feel concerned. Does a fear of dating grow and spread like mould, mildly inconvenient at first, but then so prolific in its disgusting dampness that no amount of bleach can get rid of it? I was worried that the longer I put it off, the more likely it would be that I would never date again. Becoming a crazy cat lady was out of the question because of my allergies, so it seemed I had no choice but to at least try to date again.

From the moment I accepted the invitation to the moment I pulled up at the restaurant in my mother's car a few days later, I didn't feel an ounce of excitement. At least, if I did, it was buried so deep under feelings of terror, dread, and queasiness that I didn't notice it.

As I headed towards our meeting spot, I caught a glimpse of James, standing on the corner of the street and I lost all sense of how to be a normal person.

What am I supposed to say to him? Do I hug him?

No, that can't be right. Covid, remember?

So I just smile awkwardly and say, "Hello?" That doesn't seem right!

I smiled awkwardly and said, "Hello."

Please try to act like you've socialised with other humans before.

"Hi," James said with a much more normal-looking smile. "It's nice to finally meet you."

We headed onto the cafe's terrace and took our seats under the pergola. It was a nippy afternoon, and so bleak and grey that it looked as though all of the colours had been sucked out of the world with a straw. I pulled my wrap a little tighter around me.

"It's a bit cold today," James said. Thus began the first few minutes of painfully awkward small talk. We hit all the key points – weather, traffic, Covid. "What a lovely place. Have you been here before?" It was brutal!

Taylor was right though – James was very good-looking. He was tall, broad-shouldered, and, when I dared to make eye contact, I noticed that his eyes were an unusual shade of grey-blue. His sandy hair curled around his ears and he had a warm, genuine smile. At first, he was a little stiff and timid (though nowhere near as riddled with anxiety as I was sitting across the table from him), and he was softly spoken.

By the time the waitress had come over with our drinks, the conversation was starting to flow a little more naturally and I could feel my shoulders start to relax. We chatted about which universities we'd gone to and how we'd both found ourselves living in the area. I gave the condensed version of my story, of course, opting to skirt over the failed engagement and devastating heartbreak. (It's not exactly great first date material.) I told him about my time working in Bahrain and how much I'd loved living there. He told me about a study programme he'd done in Egypt and what a fascinating experience that had been. As the afternoon wore on and the conversation twisted and turned through all sorts of topics, I realised I'd probably never met anyone I'd had so much in common with before.

"You were a literature student," he said, sipping his tea. "So who's your favourite author?"

"Dickens," I said without hesitation.

"I love Dickens!" He laughed. "His characters have so much depth."

"Yes!" I agreed. "And I love how he uses them as caricatures to highlight the flaws in society. It's pretty savage."

"Have you read any Russian literature?" He asked.

"Just *Anna Karenina* and *Crime and Punishment*.'"

"Dostoevsky is my favourite author!"

It was at that moment, as I sat across from this handsome, charming future doctor who wanted to discuss 19th-century Russian literature with me, that I realised how broken I still was. This man could not be more perfect and I could not be more desperate for the date to end.

What's the matter with me?

No matter how many compliments he gave me, how many fascinating insights he shared about Tolstoy, or how many times he repeated that he wanted nothing more than to find a nice girl to travel the world with, I just couldn't fall for this man. I just couldn't look past the fact that he was a complete stranger. He wouldn't know to put *Beauty and the Beast* on and order me a Kinder crepe when I was feeling sad. He didn't know which wine I liked to drink, or what my favourite ride at Disneyland was. He was completely and utterly perfect, but he wasn't the one I wanted. He wasn't Dylan.

I sat there and tried to imagine letting James into my life, or any man for that matter, the way that I'd let Dylan in. I tried to picture being in love with someone else and having the same wonderful times I'd had with Dylan with a new man. I couldn't.

It wasn't just the pointless remnants of love for Dylan that I was still lugging around that were holding me back from accepting someone new; there was the absolute terror, too. That afternoon, sitting outside that restaurant, I became aware of the full extent of how guarded my heart had become again. The walls were up, the drawbridge was drawn, and the moat was teeming with piranhas. I didn't want to be alone, but I didn't want to let anyone else in. It was emotional purgatory.

Just as James and I were paying the bill and getting ready to leave, huge, heavy rain droplets started to plunge down from the carpet of grey sky. In a matter of a few minutes, the scene had been transformed from a still and peaceful spring afternoon to a torrential downpour.

"Is your car parked too far away?" he asked.

"Just across the road. What about yours?"

"I only live a few streets away so I walked." I glanced out at the rain-battered streets.

"You can't walk home in this. I'll drop you off."

"No," he protested. It's no problem." I looked at him sceptically. People were ducking and diving into doorways and running for their cars. "Well," he said, following my gaze. "If you're sure you don't mind."

We raced over to my mother's car, dodging puddles and pulling our jackets up over our heads. It made no difference – we still collapsed into the car looking like drowned rats. James directed me to his house through the onslaught of rain and, a few minutes later, we pulled up outside his house.

"I've had a really lovely time with you today," he said.

"I've enjoyed it, too," I said, shifting in my now damp seat and wondering if that sounded believable. A strange, stuffy silence hung in the air for a few moments and a thought struck me.

What if he tries to kiss me?

I stared down at the steering wheel rigidly and repeated, "Yes, I enjoyed it."

Out of the corner of my eye, I saw him move rather awkwardly towards me and I sprung around almost manically. "Well, it was lovely meeting you. Bye!" I almost screamed it at him.

James smiled, looking a little startled, said goodbye and left. I took an enormous, shaky breath and pulled off. It took me a while to find my way back to the main road, especially because the relentless rain made it difficult to make sense of where I was. Finally, I found my bearings, steered myself in the direction of home … and burst into tears.

I cried with the same sudden and unexpected tenacity with which the rain had started pouring, shoulders shaking, mascara dripping down my already damp face. I wailed. My tears fell into my lap and mixed with the droplets of rain that were dripping from my damp and tangled hair. My breaths came in short, choking gasps. I cried all the way home and burst into the living room with sodden clothes and a mascara-stained face.

"Well," my mother said slowly, surveying the scene. "How was the date?"

"I don't want to go on any more dates!" I cried, throwing myself down on the sofa next to her. "It just doesn't feel right. I don't want a new man in my life. I don't even want the old one. I just want to be alone."

"That's okay," my mother said, wrapping me up in her arms like a soggy burrito. "You can just be by yourself. That's fine."

"I just feel like," I said with a sniff. "I feel like I'm not whole. There's this big, gaping space and it's awful, but I don't want to fill it with anyone else. I want to figure out how to be whole by myself."

"That sounds like the right decision," my mother said softly.

"I don't know how, though."

"Just give yourself time."

Chapter 15

"Please, please, please bless me with a parking space right next to the restaurant with plenty of room for me to pull into," I prayed frantically to the Universe.

I was meeting my friend Ava for a lunch near her home in Mumbles, a gorgeous seaside town with stunning views, quaint streets lined with pastel-coloured houses … and notoriously limited parking options. I followed the one main road through the centre of town, passing our meeting point on the left, and cursing under my breath when I saw the queue snaking out of the car park.

"Please remember that I cannot parallel park," I continued my one-sided conversation with the cosmos. "And that this car is unreasonably long. I need some help here."

Apparently, my pleas fell on deaf ears. I ended up following the stream of traffic further and further away from the restaurant until I finally found a parking space nearly a mile down the road. I stepped out of the car and looked down at the stilettos I'd squeezed my feet into. Of all the days to channel my inner real Housewife of Beverly Hills. I snatched up my bag and began the long walk back towards the restaurant, sucking in the smell of the sea air as I went.

Ava and I had met at college when we were 16 years old and were even more clueless about life than we are now. From the very beginning, I'd always been in awe of the way she could be so unapologetically herself. I marvelled at her fearlessness and downright sass and admired how she always seemed to glow with an easy confidence.

We'd had our fair share of ill-advised adventures when we were younger. We still laugh about the random house parties we sneaked into as teenagers or the time we camped out in the woods in high heels when it was five degrees outside. But somewhere along the way, life had sent us down our separate, winding paths, and we hadn't seen each other in years. She'd started a family, I'd moved overseas, Covid had forced everyone to become a hermit, and time had just slipped away. In fact, the last time I'd seen her, she'd had a toddler. Now that toddler was five years old, she'd got married and she had another baby.

By the time I finally got back to the restaurant, hobbling slightly in my shoes, Ava was already waiting outside for me. She was draped against a wall in oversized sunglasses and a faux-fur coat. It was like going to lunch with a celebrity and, in spite of the shooting pain in my calves, I decided I'd made the right decision in wearing nice shoes.

"Hi!" we both squealed in excitement.

"You look amazing!" I told her.

"Thanks," she said with a twirl. "I've given my entire wardrobe a makeover."

"Oh wow! Maybe that's something I should consider doing."

I'm already making over every element of my life.

We headed into the restaurant and took a seat on the raised terrace that overlooked the sea.

The sun's reflection sparkled amid the rise and fall of the waves, and the breeze carried the salty smell of sea air. I sat back in my seat and looked out over the view, soaking in the therapeutic sound of the lapping waves.

The waitress brought over our menus. I glanced over the drinks section for a few moments before throwing the menu back down onto the table.

"I don't know why I'm even pretending," I said. "I know it's early, but I'm going to order a glass of wine."

"I'm so glad you said that," she declared with relief. "Because so am I."

It was still fairly early on in spring, but it was an exceptionally pretty afternoon to be eating outside. The sky was clear and the delicate sunshine that poured out of the sky took the edge off the nip in the air. The food was delicious, the ever-changing view of the sea was a perfect tranquil backdrop, and the wine went down very well indeed. We sat and reminisced about the good old days when we were young and stupid, but it didn't really matter because we had no responsibilities and didn't know any better. Ava told me all about her wedding, her children, and the nightmare that was the judgey mum's club at the school gates.

"I thought I'd left all that bitchiness behind when I finished school," she said, rolling her eyes. "But then your kids go to school and you're right back where you started."

I smiled and stuffed the last of my pitta bread into my mouth. Ava looked uncomfortable all of a sudden. "Well," she said. "Are we going to talk about the elephant in the room?"

I swallowed my mouthful of bread.

"The breakup?" I asked and she nodded, taking a bite out of one of her fries. I hesitated.

"Unless you don't want to talk about it!" she said quickly.

"No, it's not that," I reassured her. "It's just that if I'm going to tell that story, then we're both going to need another glass of wine."

I regaled Ava with the unabridged version of the breakup story. She sat and listened with wide, unbelieving eyes until I'd finished, only interrupting every now and then with appropriate profanities.

"That is awful," she said when I was finished. "Are you okay now?"

"Yeah," I said honestly. "I still miss him sometimes, but I can see now that it was the best thing for both of us."

"I'm so sorry that happened to you, though."

"Do you know what? I think maybe I'm cursed in the relationship department," I laughed.

"Well, you didn't have the best start with Matt," she said and there was something like resentment in the tone of her voice. I started at the sound of his name. None of my friends had seen or spoken about Matt for years, and I was surprised to hear his name come up in conversation. It felt almost surreal after all of the time I'd spent recently, coming to terms with the things he'd said and done. Hearing someone else talk about him somehow made it all seem more real.

"Look, I feel like I need to say something," Ava said slowly, playing with the stem of her wine glass. "But I will need more wine to say what I have to say."

We ordered more wine and I watched quietly as Ava tried to think through her words.

"There's something that's been on my mind recently. Lucy is getting older and one day she's going to be a teenager and she's going to have boyfriends ..." She paused and shuddered at the thought. "I never want a guy to make her feel bad about herself. I never, ever want her to be treated badly or for her to question her worth because of anything a man says to her."

"Of course," I agreed, nodding emphatically.

She looked up at me suddenly. "I'm sorry," she said.

"For what?" I was genuinely puzzled.

"When we were in college, I knew the way that Matt treated you wasn't right. I could see it. I heard the way he used to talk to you. He was horrible to you. And some of the things he used to say about you when you weren't there were just vile. I knew it wasn't right, and it makes me feel sick because I never said anything. I didn't stand up for you or tell you to leave him. I didn't do anything."

It hurt, being catapulted back to that time again, but it was also reassuring to hear someone else validate all of the things I had begun to realise recently. A small, timid part of me had always questioned whether I'd just misremembered things. Perhaps I was just being melodramatic. After all, could it have really been that bad? It was that bad. Ava had seen it, too.

"You don't have to apologise for that," I said, shaking my head.

"I just feel awful. I was your friend. I should have said something. I should have stood up for you. I should never have let him get away with that."

"It's not your fault," I assured her.

Ava looked down in her lap and said, "I was afraid of him. I thought if I said anything, then he'd turn on me. He was so good at twisting things, and I didn't want him to say things to people … He was so manipulative!" Her brow had knitted into a frown. "I just … I wish I could go back and change it."

We sat for a second in that vulnerable silence.

"*I wish I could go back and change it* could be the unofficial tagline of my life," I said and our laughter broke the tension.

I looked across the table at Ava as she sipped her wine. She'd clearly been battling with memories of Matt for a while, just like I had. She'd been afraid of him back then, too, and all this time I'd had no idea. The girl who'd always seemed so sure of herself, so impenetrable, had been just as easily intimidated and controlled by him. It wasn't just me, then. It wasn't just because I was too weak or stupid to stick up for myself. It was him.

"You don't need to apologise for that," I repeated. "We were so young. We were so … stupid." I said and we both laughed again. "Sometimes I wish I could go back and tell my younger self all the things I know now, but she wouldn't have listened anyway. The annoying thing about experience is that you can't learn from anyone else's. You have to go through the worst of it and then think, *Hey, that was a terrible idea.* Then you dust yourself off and move on to the next terrible idea." I smiled and pushed the remnants of my food around my plate.

"I know," Ava agreed and then sighed. "I just think back over all the awful relationships I put up with. I had no standards when I was younger. I would put up with so much just because I felt like I wasn't—"

"Good enough?" I interjected and she nodded. "I understand that. It's like, you don't feel good enough so you look for that validation in a relationship, but then the guy is awful, which just confirms that you're not good enough. After a while you find yourself thinking, What *is so wrong with me that nobody treats me properly?* And then you just expect to be treated badly. It's this vicious cycle."

"Yes!' Ava burst in. "That's exactly it!"

It was strange to hear someone else give a voice to all of the same thoughts and feelings I'd been struggling to come to terms with over the last few months. I'd felt so isolated by these feelings that it had never occurred to me that I had company in them.

"I wonder how many other women feel the exact same way," I said. I took another sip of wine and sighed.

"A lot, probably." Ava made a noise of frustration and set her glass down on the table with a clank. "I don't want that to happen to Lucy. I don't want her to experience those kinds of feelings."

"She won't. You are raising her to love herself and have respect for herself. And," I added, "if any crappy men come along in the future and try to take that away from her, we will kill them."

"I'll drink to that," Ava said, laughing and we clicked our wine glasses together.

Unfortunately, a great deal of clinking had taken place that afternoon and, once we'd paid the bill and I stood up to leave, the wine really hit me.

"I'm quite drunk," I said, shocked. "I can't drive home like this."

"Well, we have had quite a few glasses of wine," Ava said, looking over the receipt. "It's fine. We'll walk to my house and you can stay there until you sober up." We got up from the table and started towards the door. Suddenly, Ava turned around and added, "Just play it cool. I don't want David to know we were getting wine drunk at 12 o'clock while he was home with the kids."

It was a short but meandering walk back to Ava's house, and we both did our best to appear completely sober as we walked up the garden path. Unfortunately, our rendition of "completely sober" must not have been too convincing.

"Hello!" Ava said as we walked through the door.

"Are you two drunk?" Ava's husband asked with a small smile the moment we stumbled into the kitchen.

"No!" we said in an unconvincing chorus.

"Ladies," he said, looking down at his watch. "You've been at lunch for four hours."

I stayed in Ava's house for the next few hours, sipping water and waiting for the wine fog to lift. I chatted with her little girl, and tried (and failed) to understand the concept of Fortnite as she talked me through it. I cooed over her baby boy as he rolled around on the living room floor, sticking his fingers into everything and smiling at his feet. Sitting there, in the midst of this little family, I felt a pang of regret. If things had worked out differently, this is what I could have had – the home, the husband the adorable children.

What do you have now? You're 30, single, and you live with your parents.

Actually, I'm not accepting unnecessary criticism at this time. I'm doing my best and that's enough.

Chapter 16

I was busy throwing every ounce of energy I had into rebuilding myself and trying to stack together the building blocks of a new foundation for my life. Whenever my emotions began to bubble up towards the brim again, I'd write them all down. It was like opening a pressure release valve in my brain. As the negativity slowly seeped out of my life, I recalled Sophie's advice about finding things I enjoyed. I decided to fill the empty space where those difficult emotions had been with positivity instead.

I'd always wanted to learn to sew, so I dusted off my old sewing machine and began to spend my evenings piecing together a quilt. The seams weren't quite right and at one point I accidentally sewed a pin into one of the patchwork squares, but when I held up the finished product at the end, I smiled with a sense of pride. I wanted to achieve more. So I ordered a set of crochet hooks on Amazon and taught myself to make a cardigan. Then I knitted a jumper. Before long, I set up an Etsy shop and found myself stitching and knitting into the early hours of the morning. I was tired, but also glowing with the satisfaction of everything I was accomplishing.

I was still going to dance lessons, but I decided that I wanted to train to run a five-k too. I'd never run before in my life. In fact, I still get flashbacks from secondary-school PE lessons. Nevertheless, I threw myself into it and started running three evenings a week.

Before long I was cramming my days full of "positivity". I devoured self-help books and poured personal development podcasts into my ears morning, noon, and night. I took up yoga. I wrote in my journal and meditated daily. I started learning Spanish again. I filled every minute of every day with something productive that would occupy my brain or body. I was so frantically positive that, from the outside looking in, it must have looked like I had joined some kind of cult.

For a while, it seemed to be working, though. I barely had the time or mental capacity left over to dwell on negativity and all of my energy was focused on myself. I convinced myself that every hour spent on learning a new skill or pushing myself to run that little bit faster or reading a new book was a special form of self-care. I was giving myself the tools I needed to move forwards. I was showering myself with time and attention. Surely that was the route to self-love and acceptance.

Once again, I was simply quite deluded.

One morning, at the height of this period of intense soul-searching and my impassioned commitment to all things personal development, I logged onto a video call with Sophie. As usual, the session started with a brief overview of how I was doing and what, if anything, had happened since we'd last spoken. I gripped my mug of green tea, taking sporadic sips between my excited explanation about all of the positive things I had been doing recently. Sophie watched me through the screen, nodding and listening patiently as I rambled on about how productive I was being, how many exciting new projects I had on the go, and how I was implementing yoga to help reduce my anxiety.

"Right," she said when I was finally finished. "And is it working?" I took another frenzied sip of tea.

"Yes!" I insisted. "I feel like I'm finally becoming this new, improved version of myself."

"Is that important?" she asked simply. I faltered for a second, sensing that she was about to hit me with a curveball. I racked my brain for the correct answer to her question. I didn't for a second stop to think about the irony of my trying so intently to "win" at a coaching session that was orchestrated to support my own mental health.

"Well, yes," I said, more slowly and, in the pause that followed, I could practically hear the cogs in my brain turning, scratching around for clues as to where I'd gone wrong.

"Do you need to be a new, improved version of yourself?" she asked.

"Well, I want to feel better. I want to feel good about myself," I said with a conviction I no longer actually felt.

"And you can't feel good about yourself the way you are?"

The point came crashing down on me with such force that it knocked all those straining cogs into disarray for a few moments and all I could do was sit and settle into the discomfort of her words. Was that what was happening here? All these weeks I'd spent devoting my time and energy to "becoming my best self" – was I only doing that because, deep down, I still didn't think the person I already was, was *good enough* to deserve happiness?

"Maybe," I started, struggling with this new idea, "I thought that if I was 'better', I would feel happier."

"*Do* you feel happier doing all of these things?" Sophie asked, clearly already knowing the answer.

"No!" I admitted. I let the curtain of pretence fall from my face. "I still feel stressed and overwhelmed and miserable! Like with the yoga! I get so flustered by it because I keep telling myself that it should make me calm, but then I just get stressed about the fact that I'm *not calm*. What kind of a person stresses about how stressed yoga makes them? What's wrong with me?" The words tumbled out all at once. Green tea sloshed over the side of my mug and onto my lap.

"Okay," Sophie said in a soothing voice. "Take a big breath in. And then out." We did a few rounds of deep breathing and then she said, "Now repeat after me: I am enough."

"I am enough," I repeated quietly.

"Now louder and like you mean it."

"I am enough." I shifted uncomfortably in my seat.

Sophie encouraged me to repeat those three words over and over before finally asking, "Now how do you feel?"

"Like it isn't true," I said and I was suddenly aware of the tears sliding down my cheeks.

There it was – that unshakable sense of inferiority again. Each time I tried to force those three simple words out of my mouth, I felt the sting of it.

"That's your new affirmation," Sophie told me. "I want you to say it all day long. Say it when you wake up. Say it when you're at your desk. Say it when you're in the shower. The more you say it, the more you'll start to realise it's true."

After that conversation, everything changed. It was as if a crucial puzzle piece had finally clicked into place – the kind that suddenly changes the entire picture.

Oh, wait! This jigsaw is a picture of an adorable puppy, not a feral raccoon. How silly of me!

Suddenly, it all made sense. This idea that I wasn't enough had caused the nagging sensation of emptiness that I'd always been unable to shake off. I'd tried, desperately, to fill that void with other things – the fancy apartment, the exciting job, the far-flung trips, the "perfect" fiancé. But none of those things had ever been able to stave off that feeling that something was missing for long. Nothing would ever be able to fill up that hole inside of me except for the love and respect that I needed to give *to myself*.

Then I was able to understand that that young girl who deep down didn't believe she was good enough, really *had* been a beacon for gaslighters and liars all along. Who else would have put up with them? How could she have expected to be treated well by others when she didn't believe she deserved it herself? And, when she'd finally found a man who had treated her with genuine love and respect, she'd clung to him as if her life depended on him because he made up for the fact that she felt completely unable to give those things to herself.

My worth has nothing to do with anybody else.

It was a revelation that struck me like lightning and left me reeling in its simplicity. All this time, I'd been so worried about how I would possibly begin to rebuild myself after so much of me felt like it had been torn away. Suddenly it was obvious. Those parts that were gone weren't necessary because they didn't come from me. I didn't need to carry the scars of Matt's hurtful words or depend on Dylan's love and care to give me a sense of stability. I didn't need to build the foundation of myself on anyone else's opinion of me. I already had all the pieces I needed to rebuild my sense of self. I just needed to be … *myself!* And that was enough.

After that life-coaching session with Sophie, I looked at myself in the mirror every day and told myself, "I am enough."

I said it when I first woke up, I whispered it to myself while I was driving to work, repeated it over and over in my head, and saved it as the lock screen on my phone. At first, the words felt hollow. I didn't *feel* enough. I wasn't organised and I wasn't a morning person. I was still struggling to run five kilometres after months of training. My jeans didn't fit and my skin was a disaster.

"I am enough," I persisted, day after day.

It didn't feel true. I was 29 years old and living in my parents' spare room. I had no set career path, and my judgement was clearly flawed at best. I had panic attacks at least once a week.

"I am enough," I told myself through tears and gritted teeth.

Sophie was right. It took some time, but slowly those three words helped to plant the seed of self-worth in the empty space inside me. Every time I chose to ignore my self-doubts and counter all my fears with "I am enough", that self-worth grew stronger. It took time, but eventually I realised that I really was enough.

Chapter 17

One afternoon, just as spring was melting into summer, I did something impulsive and out of character. I bought an online tarot reading. Tarot, reiki, psychics, astrology – it had all always been outside of my realm of interest. For all I knew, a root chakra was a kind of herb used in Italian seasoning. Now here I was adding a virtual tarot reading to my online shopping cart.

No seriously – who the heck am I?

It had all started a few weeks before when Kellie from work handed me a small but hugely impactful gift. I'd shuffled into work that morning with glazed, purple-ringed eyes. Despite all of the progress I'd made and all of the mental poison I'd managed to suck out of my wounds, my body was still struggling to recover. Sleep was still elusive and I was wrung out by ten months' worth of long, sleepless nights. I was still tense with anxiety, too, and the constant nausea made it difficult to pick through my food.

On a more positive note, my eyelashes had finally started to grow back.

I tramped up the stairs to the classroom and each step in my heavy boots felt like an enormous effort. I unlocked the door, flipped on the lights, and headed straight towards the kettle, shaking off my jacket.

I collapsed into the nearest chair and sipped on my second cup of coffee of the morning. Before long, I heard the echoing clang of footsteps on the metal stairwell outside the door, closely followed by the sound of Shannon's voice.

"Good morning," she said with a smile, unzipping her jacket.

"Good morning," I croaked.

Kellie was a tarot card reader, and training to become a reiki healer. She was softly spoken and empathetic and, when I first met her, I was immediately drawn to (and sometimes somewhat puzzled by) her unique view of the world. Once, when I'd told her that I'd been suffering from insomnia, she'd cocked her head to one side and asked me simply if I'd considered calling on my angel guides for protection.

"No," I'd said slowly. "I've just been taking the sleeping pills my doctor prescribed."

I could open up to Kellie about anything without judgement. No matter what the topic of conversation, she was able to see things from a new perspective I'd never considered before. I enjoyed listening to her philosophical points of view and, the more time I'd spent with her, the more intrigued I'd become by this magical-sounding world she seemed to live in.

"I have a gift for you." She smiled shyly as she made her way into the classroom. I raised my eyebrows in surprise. "It's just something small," she added quickly. "Maybe it's a bit random, but I saw it and I felt like you needed to have it. I don't know … Maybe that sounds crazy."

She slipped her hand into her pocket and pulled out a smooth orange-brown stone. She placed it in the palm of my hand and I rolled it around in my fingers. The smooth surface was cool on my skin.

"Thank you," I said, feeling truly grateful for the gift, even though I had no idea what it was.

"It's red jasper," she told me, taking a seat across from me. "You said you wanted to learn a bit more about crystals."

"That's so kind of you," I said, turning the stone over in my hand.

"All crystals have powers," she explained. "But I honestly don't know what red jasper is used for. It may not even resonate with you. I just felt like this one was for you somehow."

"Let's Google it," I suggested.

Kellie made herself a coffee and we sat together on the sofa as I did a quick Google search on red jasper.

It turns out that red jasper can be used to increase:

- Self-esteem
- Emotional stamina
- Feelings of calm and relaxation
- Emotional wellbeing

"Honestly," I said after reading the list out loud to Shannon. "I think this is the most appropriate gift anyone's ever given me."

That night, I popped the little, round stone on my bedside table as I got into bed, and felt an immediate sense of calm. Maybe the polished hunk of red jasper really did have mood-altering powers. Maybe it was a really excellent placebo. Maybe it was just an effective visual reminder that things were getting better and that I had the support around me to help me through the rest of this healing process. Either way, I slipped into a relatively peaceful sleep that night and woke up the next morning illuminated by a sense of renewed positivity.

After that, I did what many millennial women in a state of emotional crisis find themselves doing – I spent a whole bunch of money on crystals. I had clear quartz on a necklace and rose quartz stashed in the glove box of my car. I kept a piece of amethyst on my bedside table next to my red jasper, and soon added malachite and citrine to the crew. It was never my intention to become a crazy crystal lady, but their presence throughout my space was reassuring. I linked each stone with a positive affirmation or promise to myself, so that every time I walked into my room or started my car or put my hand in my bag (because yes, I also kept a stash of crystals there, too), I was reminded that I was a kick-ass woman and I was going to be okay.

Etsy was quick to pick up on my new obsession, and each time I opened the site, shiny new crystal necklaces and gift sets would pop up as recommended items. Then, one day, as I was scrolling through pictures of rose quartz rings, I saw the recommended listing for an online tarot reading. I instinctively stopped and let my laptop's cursor hover over the listing. For some reason, I was just drawn to it.

You don't believe in tarot readings, remember?

I stared at the screen and wondered whether I was actually considering this for real. I'd come a long way in the last few months. I had a growing sense of self-belief and I finally felt like I was going to be all right. The unavoidable sticking point was that I still had no idea where I was going. The huge grey cloud around me had started to thin, but there was still no sign of a viable path to follow. I had no idea what I was meant to do next and that unknowing was like an unbearable itch that I just couldn't scratch.

If looking down at a little hunk of clear quartz on a chain around my neck at the power to remind me that I was a confident, capable woman, then maybe a tarot reading would have the power to ease some of this stress about the future.

Even if it is just all a placebo effect, what difference does it make if it makes me feel better?

That's how I came to add the virtual tarot reading to my Etsy cart one afternoon. I filled in the online form, revealing as little information about myself as I possibly could for scepticism's sake. In the space for questions and queries, I wrote a little note expressing a need for clarity about what I should do now.

Actually, any kind of clarity would be great right now.

The response arrived two days later while I was at work and I had to wait, impatiently, through an afternoon that seemed to stretch on forever, before I could rush home and open it. I ran straight up to my room in a flurry of excited anticipation. I clicked the link in the email and my video tarot reading popped up on the screen (I know – how very 21st century). I watched intently, hunched down over the screen, as May, the tarot reader, began to shuffle the deck. Ten cards suddenly burst out of the pack and scattered everywhere.

I'm no expert, but I think the Universe may have something to say.

One after another, the cards flashed up in front of me on the screen – the twin flame, the soulmates, and the lovers. I sat in confused silence and listened as May sighed.

"I'm getting a vibe from this," she said. "But I just want to check."

She pulled out another card from another deck and I squinted to see what it said. Below a small drawing of a mirror were the words, *Relationships reflect our wounds.*

Well, ain't that the truth?

"It seems like you've had a relationship and maybe you've struggled to move on," May explained. "It's a hard one to read because at first, it looked like maybe there was a twin flame connection between you, but it's not that. It's not necessarily the person you're holding onto. You're struggling to let go, because this relationship was meant to teach you a really difficult lesson." I listened, wide-eyed, as this eerily accurate picture continued to unfold. "In order to let go and truly learn this lesson, you need to learn to love yourself."

I sat back, amazed but a little frustrated. It was all I could do not to shout, *I know that but how?* at the screen.

May began shuffling the cards again. Then she pulled out a new card from within the deck. Underneath a brightly coloured picture in hues of pink and purple were gold words that read, *A year from now.* The words struck me for no particular reason.

"That doesn't really answer your question of what you should do now," May said apologetically. "Let me try again." She shuffled the deck for the final time and a single card fluttered free from the rest. I watched through the screen as May picked it up and held it towards the camera. It was the exact same card that read *A year from now.*

"I think you're not meant to focus your energy on what's going on right now," May explained. "To me, this seems like you should be focussing on what's going to happen a year from now."

The video ended and I sat back on my heels, pondering over everything I had just read.

What the heck is going to happen a year from now?

Let's be honest, anything could happen in a year's time. This time last year you were newly engaged and about to move to California.

The realisation slowly began to fan out in front of me. My life had changed so dramatically and so unexpectedly over the course of a single year. Unfortunately, that change had been less than preferable. But what was to stop my life from changing dramatically for the better over the course of the next year? Maybe instead of obsessing over my next immediate step, I needed a longer-term goal. If I could just take all of my attention off the tree that was blocking my path, I'd realise there was an enormous forest of opportunity all around me.

If I had learned anything throughout my healing process (other than the fact that I was enough and that *The Greatest Showman* soundtrack is a dangerous tear-jerker after too many glasses of wine), it was that change was gradual. It required persistent work and a great deal of time. I knew what I wanted for myself in this new life I was building, but I wasn't going to achieve those things overnight. I could start working towards them, little by little, and achieve them by this time next year or this time next year could roll around and I could be in the exact same spot I was in now, waiting for a sense of clarity that would probably never come.

Heading in the right general direction is better than standing still just because I haven't got the whole path mapped out yet.

I processed all of this information in the days following my tarot reading. Then, one morning, a pulled out some coloured pens and a notebook, and started creating a plan. I made a list of all of the things I wanted in my life by this time next year with the caveat that they all had to be things that came from within me. I was finished with searching for fulfilment in external things. Instead of a fancy car or a new fiancé, I filled the list with words like "happiness", "healthiness", and "creativity".

Now how do I get to where I want to be by this time next year? One day at a time, I guess.

So I took it one day at a time. Each day I did one thing would edge me closer to those things I'd set my mind on achieving by the time another year had rolled around. Now I felt like I had a sense of purpose and control. I had a rough path to follow and it didn't even really matter what the destination looked like once I got there. My goals were all centred on me and not the stuff I'd tried chasing in the past. If I was happy, healthy, creative, and made time for the things I loved to do most, who cared where I lived or what kind of job I did. If I stopped hanging my happiness on things outside of myself, I'd find that sense of steady contentment that Sophie had talked about.

I started to notice a significant change in myself after that. It was as if I had finally been handed back the reins to my own life and I felt able to steer myself through it. As the next few weeks went by, I continued to do one thing every day that aligned with my goals. Those small actions started to stack up. My confidence continued to grow. I could already feel that my life was changing for the better.

Chapter 18

The next time I spoke to Sophie during one of our video sessions, I had plenty of good news to share with her. I told her about all of the positive daily steps I'd been taking to change my life for the better. Then I went on to tell her how much my confidence had bloomed since I'd started reminding myself each day that I was enough.

"I feel better," I said with a relieved smile.

"I'm glad. I've been telling you for all these months how capable you are, and now I think you're finally seeing it for yourself."

When she asked how I was feeling about Dylan, I could tell her with complete honesty that I was okay.

"I'm still sad sometimes," I admitted. "I don't know if that's because I miss Dylan, or just because I miss my old life. But I also don't want my old life back, if that makes sense. I spent so much time wishing Dylan and I could figure it out and get back together, but now I can see that the relationship wasn't right. We're different people. We want different things. I don't want to go back to that. Now I just want to move on with my life and leave it all in the past."

"And what's preventing you from leaving it in the past now?" Sophie asked. "It sounds like you're in the right headspace to let it all go. What's stopping you?"

"He's still got my stuff," I told her, and I watched her eyes widen through the screen.

"Still?" she said in disbelief. "I thought you said he was going to post it back to you months ago."

"He told me he was going to a few weeks after I posted my ring back …" I winced at the memory of it, remembering the sting of that blow. Dylan had sent me a text message a few weeks after the breakup, asking me to post my engagement ring back to him in California. I'd had to stuff the symbol of all my hopes and dreams into a cardboard box and return it as if it were a faulty Amazon order. It tore me apart at the time, and even bringing it up with Sophie all those months later made my heart ache.

"So why hasn't he sent it?" Sophie's face, which was usually composed into a calm expression, free of judgement, was screwed up in confusion.

"Well," I sighed, "he said he took it to the Post Office, but the shipping was too expensive. He told me he was going to squeeze it all into a smaller box and see if that was cheaper."

"And?"

"And then he said it was still too expensive, so he was going to try a different Post Office."

"A different Post Office?" Sophie repeated.

"The thing is," I said, starting to feel irritation rise up within me, "I told him to just let me know the cost and I'd transfer him the money. What difference does it make to him how much it costs if I'm the one paying for it?" I sighed again, a little more angrily this time.

"Is this the only thing the two of you stay in contact about?" Sophie asked.

"Yes."

"So this stuff is the final tie between the two of you. Once you get it back, there won't be any reason for you to speak to him again."

"Yes. That's why I want it back! Once I have my stuff, that will be my closure."

Sophie considered this for a second, and then asked, "Do you think you could get the same kind of closure from sending him a message and telling him you don't want the stuff anymore? Tell him he can donate it or throw it away or … whatever. Then there's no more stuff, no more tie between the two of you, and you'll be able to leave this in the past without having to wait for it to be on his terms."

I frowned. I wanted my stuff back. It was only a small box of things that I'd taken to California the last time I visited to get a head-start on moving. It was mostly clothing, but there were a couple of sentimental items in there and one particularly expensive cocktail dress that I'd had custom made for me. Other than the few special things in there, everything was replaceable. What Sophie was saying made sense. This could be an opportunity for me to take control of the situation and end it once and for all, on my terms. It was a logical solution.

"No," I told her, shaking my head petulantly. "I want my stuff back!"

"Why is it so important to you? You've gone without it for this long."

"Because ..." I started, realising I had no idea what the answer to that question was. Then, from some dark recess of my brain, it appeared. "Because he's already taken everything else from me. He doesn't get to keep this, too!"

I sat, blinking in the wake of this new revelation. It wasn't the stuff that was important to me. It was the principle. Some small, injured part of me was still keeping score. He had walked away from our relationship and into the exact life he'd wanted. The only thing he'd lost was me, and he was quick enough to find my replacement. I'd walked away with no job, no apartment, no self-respect, and no idea how to start over. In what world was it fair that he should get to keep my stuff, too?

Wow. Where was all of that hiding?

"Okay," Sophie said. "I can understand why you feel that way. But if you hang onto this stuff and stop it from letting you move on, then he's taking a lot more away from you than a few dresses and some souvenirs. At the moment, this fight over the stuff is stealing some of your happiness. It's keeping you stuck in this place, waiting for him to decide when it ends. It may not be what feels right at the moment, but I think the best thing you can do is to take back your power and end it for yourself."

When the call ended, I sat and thought back over what Sophie had said. She was right, of course. Attaching so much meaning and emotion and power to a bunch of junk I hadn't even laid eyes on in over a year was unnecessary. It was holding me back, keeping me stuck in a strange sense of limbo. I needed to be the one who cut that final tie.

I picked up my phone and began typing out a message to Dylan, telling him to donate my stuff to Goodwill. Then I deleted it. I slid my phone across the table, put my head in my hands, and sighed. Today was not that day.

Chapter 19

I shuffled through the narrow aisle of the plane, trying my best not to knock my backpack against every single seat-back I passed as I went. I found my seat and lifted the bag up into the overhead compartment. Then I took my seat next to the window and smiled to myself underneath my face mask. It felt incredible to be boarding a plane again.

Usually, flying filled me with nothing but dread and brain-frying levels of stress. After all, the whole process is so unpleasant. First, you have to haul all your luggage to the airport. Then there are the queues to check in, and the inevitability of being forced to walk through security in nothing but your socks while juggling a plastic bag full of liquids that refuses to stay sealed shut. There's a brief time of calm in which you can purchase an insanely overpriced coffee in the departure lounge. Then you queue again to board a giant tin can that launches you through the air while the person next to you hogs the armrest. That's all followed up with being elbowed back off the plane by overly eager fellow passengers and queuing yet again at passport control.

The frequent flying I'd done in the past, shuttling between Bahrain, the UK, and California, hadn't done anything to ease my discomfort. Weirdly, the more I flew, the more stressed the prospect of flying made me. But this time felt different. I'd stepped out of the car with my suitcase and gazed up at the ugly exterior of the airport like it was an old friend. I savoured the feeling of my boarding pass in my hand, and beamed my way through the Tetris game of a security check. Stepping onto a plane after so many months of border closures and travel bans felt downright invigorating. I'd never been more excited to hear a flight safety announcement.

I was finally about to embark on my mini Eat, Pray, Love adventure. Well, technically I was just doing the Eat part (which, as we all know, is the best part anyway). On the same day that the Covid travel ban was lifted, I messaged Nick and asked him when I could visit him in Naples. I booked the flight that same afternoon, and here I was, a few weeks later, on my way to eat my weight in carbs.

I sat back in my seat and glanced out of the window. People were busy flinging suitcases into the luggage hold of the plane next to ours. The last time I'd boarded a plane was when I'd flown home wearing my new engagement ring to visit my parents for a few weeks. Nearly an entire year had passed since then, and every single aspect of my life had changed. I had hit rock bottom and I'd bounced back up again. Well, maybe I hadn't bounced exactly. I'd crawled slowly and clumsily, and veered off track a few times along the way. The main thing was, I was finally starting to feel like myself again.

No, that wasn't quite right. I didn't feel like my old self, because I wasn't her anymore. I'd pieced together the broken shards of the old me who had survived the fall and I'd filled in all the empty spaces with self-love. I was full of a sense of confidence that I hadn't felt in years.

The familiar clunking noises from behind me told me that the cabin crew had begun the process of closing the door. I adjusted my face mask and craned my neck to survey the plane. Including me, there were fewer than a dozen people on board. There were empty rows all around me, and one cabin crew member was busy reassigning seats to "balance the weight of the plane". It would appear that travel was legal again, but that most people weren't crazy enough to throw themselves onto the first flight they could find leaving the country.

A few hours later, I was heaving my case off the luggage carousel. I was a little frizzy and dishevelled after standing in the sticky queue at passport control, but I didn't let the clamminess dampen my excitement. I stepped outside into the warm evening air and the raucous chatter of the world outside the airport. A mess of cars was parked at peculiar angles across the carpark and people stood amid it all, calling loudly to one another. I squinted into the evening, scouring the scene for Nick.

"Hey!" came the only voice I knew that could possibly carry over the din. "Aimée!"

I waded through the chaos to where Nick was standing beside his car. "Hi!" I beamed as he wrapped me up in a tight hug. I looked up at his smiling face and was hit square in the chest with an unexpected wave of nostalgia.

It had been such a strange, emotionally draining year. Lockdown had given life an air of unreality, and everything had slipped into a hazy, muddled confusion. My time in Bahrain – that part of my life that I had loved so much – had started to seem like a far-off dream. Hearing Nick's rambunctious laugh as he squeezed me in a hug gave it substance again. It had been real. All of that had actually happened!

Nick tossed my suitcase into the boot of his car and we began the winding journey up to his house in Pozzuoli. I watched the yellow lights of the lampposts streak by and tried to pick out some of the passing scenery in the darkness. Nick and I caught up during the drive.

"Julia is excited to meet you," he told me.

"I'm excited to meet her, too," I said with a smile.

Nick's newest love interest *("She's not my girlfriend – don't call her that!")* had come to visit from Spain. Our trips only overlapped by a few days, but I was looking forward to spending what little time I could getting to know her.

"It sucks she's not staying longer so you'd have someone to hang out with while I'm at work next week."

"I'm sure I'll be able to keep myself entertained," I said, and then suddenly remembered something. "Did my package come yet?"

Nick shook his head apologetically.

"Seriously?" I groaned. "Dylan told me he was sending it weeks ago. How is it still not here?"

"I'm sure it'll get here before you leave," Nick said.

In spite of Sophie's suggestion that I get over it and simply let it go, Dylan and I were still tangled up in the negotiation over my stuff. Each trip he made to the Post Office was followed up with an apologetic text message about how expensive the postage was.

"It's fine," I would tell him. *"I'll just transfer you the money for it."*

It was Nick who'd suggested that Dylan send the package directly to Nick's FPO address in Italy. That would finally put an end to the cost of shipping drama we'd been tangled up in for all these months. I could get the package from Nick while I was visiting, and that final string tying me to the past would be undone.

"I hope it gets here in time," I said to Nick, but deep down I already knew it would never arrive.

Nick's house was nestled on a mountainside, inside a small gated community. The drive up the steep, winding slopes almost made me dizzy. The road looped around in a puzzling series of one-way streets, most of which seemed almost hidden in the dark. Eventually, we arrived at the tall metal gates and Nick pulled the car slowly into a little covered driveway outside his house. By the time we arrive, it was almost midnight.

We dragged my suitcase down the stone steps that led to the porch, and Nick threw open the front door theatrically.

"Ta-da!" he said, flicking on the flights to reveal the open-plan kitchen and living room. Nick's huge gaming chair sat in the centre of the room facing an enormous TV and outrageously expensive sound system. Everything else in the room seemed modest in comparison. It was clearly the home of an unmarried man in his early twenties.

"So, you've got your priorities right," I laughed.

"Well, most of the time I'm the only one here, so I don't really need a lot of furniture."

"I see the logic," I said, nodding.

He gave me a brief tour of the house, and I set my suitcase down in the guest bedroom.

"That bed is so comfortable," he told me proudly. "Julia and I put it together yesterday. She's probably outside, waiting for us."

He led me back out of the house and into the stone porch. Then he pointed to the left, where a slim, metal gate sat at the end of a long passage. I gave the gate a push and stepped through onto the terrace.

It was unbelievable. The town stretched out below us, discernible only by the thousands of tiny lights that flickered in the darkness. I looked out at the faintest outlines of buildings that were scattered haphazardly along the mountainside and squinted to see how they eventually melted into the darkness below. Further out, the view was dominated by the blackness of the sea, which was lit, in one small spot, by the rippling reflection of the moon on the waves.

I turned back to Nick in disbelief. "Wow!"

"I know!" he boomed. "The view is why I chose this house."

"Wait until you see it in the daylight," came a voice from the other side of the terrace. "Hi, I'm Julia." Nick's newest girlfriend walked over with a timid smile. Even in the dim yellow light of the fire pit that burned in the centre of the terrace, I could see she was pretty. Her long, thick hair was pulled back in a loose bun, and her big, dark eyes glistened in the glow of the fire. Her thick Spanish accent made her words sound musical.

I introduced myself to Julia and we sat down by the fire. Nick pulled out his phone and ordered us some food from the nearby pizzeria. While he was trying to decipher the Italian menu and Julia was pouring us all glasses of wine, I took a picture of the view and added it to my Instagram story. A few minutes later, my phone rang.

I looked up at Nick in surprise. "It's Dylan," I said, confused.

"Why is he calling you?" he asked and I shrugged in response. I answered the phone and headed to the other end of the balcony. The crickets chirped loudly.

"Hello?"

"Hey," came the familiar voice from the other end of the phone. "How's Italy?"

"Yeah, it's good," I said, leaning against a wall and looking back out towards the sea. "I only just got here really, but it's nice to see Nick."

"Good," he said, and then, after a pause, he added, "I just wanted to let you know about your package. I took it to the Post Office today and tried to send it to Nick's address, but it actually worked out more expensive than sending it to the UK."

"Really? But FPO addresses are supposed to have free postage, aren't they? Nick said his mothers sends him stuff here all the time and she doesn't pay anything."

"Yeah, that's what I thought too, but I guess not. I can take it back to the Post Office tomorrow and try again. Maybe the lady there was just confused."

"Thanks," I said, disappointed. "I appreciate it."

"No problem."

When the phone call was over, I headed back to the fire pit and sat down heavily next to Julia.

"What was that about?" asked Nick.

"He couldn't send the package," I said with a shrug. "It was too expensive."

Nick screwed his face up in an expression of confusion blended with disbelief. "But it's supposed to be free!"

I shrugged again in response and picked my glass of wine up off the table.

"Would you like me to try to talk to him about it?" Nick asked. "I mean, why wouldn't he want to send it?"

"It's okay. I actually don't really care anymore."

I sat back in my seat and took a sip of wine, watching the moonlight dance across the surface of the black water below us. All the time I'd been so focussed on my reasons for wanting to get the stuff back that I'd never stopped to wonder what Dylan's reasons were for not sending it. Nick's question had thrown light on something I'd never considered before. Maybe Dylan couldn't bring himself to cut that final string either.

At the end of the month, it would be a year since the breakup. It was definitely time for us to become unsevered from each other. For both of our sakes, I would have to put my pettiness aside and be the one to cut that last remaining tie.

A part of me was sad to know that I would be losing some treasured possessions, but it was worth it to do what was right for both of us. At that moment, I decided to let go of my end of the string. I gave up the stuff. I gave up on the principle of the matter. And I realised, in doing so, that letting go was actually far easier than holding on.

Dylan didn't get back to me the next day with an update from the Post Office. In fact, without me ever telling him that I no longer wanted them, he never made another attempt to send my things back to me. I have no idea how much longer he held onto his end of the string, but that night in Italy, I felt relieved to finally be untethered and able to continue to move forwards without looking back.

Chapter 20

Nick was right – the new guest mattress was very comfortable. So comfortable, in fact, that I slept right through the night and the entire morning, too. I finally drifted back into consciousness in the early afternoon. I rolled over in the giant marshmallow of a mattress, picked up my phone, and gasped out loud when I saw the time. I couldn't remember the last time I'd slept through the night, let alone through most of the next day.

There was a new message from Nick waiting for me on my phone. It said that he and Julia had gone out to pick up some groceries, but that he'd left some coffee in the top cupboard for me.

He knows me so well.

I rolled out of bed and stumbled into the kitchen, still shaking off the blurriness of sleep. I grabbed the jar of coffee from the top shelf and surveyed the kitchen counters hopefully. There was no sign of a kettle, which broke my little British heart, but microwaved coffee was better than no coffee at all.

I started opening up the other cupboards one by one in search of a mug. All I found were a couple of pots and pans that looked like they'd never been used, a few pieces of cutlery, four plates, and a stack of disposable plastic cups. That was the full extent of it. I stared, bleary-eyed and confused at the scare assortment of kitchenware.

I pulled my phone out of my pocket and sent Nick a message.

Me: *Do you have any mugs?*

Nick: *LOL! No! I didn't even think about that. I'll get one at the store. Use my flask that's on the counter.*

Smiling to myself, I rolled my eyes and pulled one of the shiny pans out of the cupboard. It truly was a bachelor's kitchen. I poured some water into the pan and began the ridiculous procedure of making coffee without a kettle or a mug. Quite a lot of it ended up sloshing into the sink as I tried to carefully transfer it from the pan into the narrow mouth of Nick's flask, but I'd salvaged enough to give me the caffeine fix I needed.

I snatched up the flask and a leftover slice of pizza before heading out onto the terrace. Julia was right – the view was even more amazing during the day. Now that it was light, the luscious, deep green of the trees was visible between the boxy white houses that trailed down the mountainside and eventually levelled out onto the flat ground below. The rich, blue sky melted into the deep grey-blue of the sea on the horizon. Off to the left-hand side, a squat, dumpy stone of a mountain rose up out of the water. I sat down with my coffee and stared out at the view.

The sound of Nick's car pulling into the little covered driveway snapped me out of my sleepy trance around 20 minutes later. I headed back into the house to help Nick and Julia unpack the groceries.

"How did you sleep?" Julia asked. My hair was knotted in a mess on top of my head and I hadn't bothered to put on any makeup. I probably looked as though I wasn't entirely awake yet.

"Actually, I can't remember the last time I slept that well," I told her.

"I told you it was an awesome mattress!" said Nick enthusiastically.

"Where are the new mugs?" Julia asked and Nick produced a long box out of one of the bags.

"I got four of them," he told me proudly.

Julia opened the box and immediately rolled her eyes. "Nick!" she cried in her beautiful accent. "These are not coffee mugs!" She thrust her hand into the box and pulled something out. It looked like a coffee mug … for a child's tea set. "These are for espressos!"

"Oh," said Nick, looking genuinely surprised.

"It's fine," I laughed. "As long as I get my caffeine in the morning, I'm not really too bothered what form it comes in."

After we put away the groceries, we headed back out onto the terrace, dragging the garden furniture into the shade to escape the intense heat of the sun.

"It's a shame you have to go back to Spain tonight," I told Julia. "It would have been nice for us to have had more time to get to know each other."

"Yes. I wish I was staying longer. Do you have any plans for while you're here?"

I shook my head. "Not really. I have to self-isolate for the next few days, which is going to be a bit boring, especially because Nick is going to be at work all day. I'll probably just do some writing and work on my tan until I'm allowed out to explore."

"I think that sounds like a good plan," Julia said with a smile.

That night, just before midnight, I hugged Julia goodbye as Nick lugged her suitcase up the short flight of stone steps to his car. I waved goodbye to her from the entryway.

"Have a safe flight!"

"Thank you. Have an amazing time," she said with a final wave.

Unfortunately, my amazing time had to be postponed until after my self-isolation period was over.

I relished my first few days in such a gorgeous mountain-top house in Pozzuoli. I spent as much time as I could out on the terrace. I would wake up and shuffle out there with my coffee (alternating between using Nick's flask and one of the tiny espresso cups). Then I'd spend the warm and hazy mornings draped over a chair with a book, or jabbing away at the keys of my laptop, busily adding more and more to my story, which by then I'd decided would eventually become a book. Then, as the sun climbed higher in the sky, I'd retreat back into the shade, dragging my little chair further and further into the corner of the terrace to evade the blazing heat.

By lunchtime, the sun would peek down from the cloudless sky and find me in my corner, baring down with such an intensity that I had no option but to go back inside. I'd flit between indoors and outdoors all day long. I was desperate to sit out on that terrace and enjoy the sights and the sunshine, but I could only manage to stay out there for 20 minutes at a time while the sun was beating down. After that, I'd retire back into the house, sweaty and a little starry-eyed and pink.

In the evenings, I would catch up with Nick and revel in a bit of human company. We watched some films, drank more wine and covered the most random topics of conversation. The was a warm and soothing familiarity in his company. It was like no time had elapsed since we'd last sat in my apartment in Bahrain, stuffing our faces with takeaway food with Dylan and Nina.

It was a lovely, relaxing way to while away a few days. The remnants of my stress melted away under the glistening gaze of the sunshine. I slept soundly in the comfortable guest bed and made steady progress with my writing.

But by day four, I was starting to lose my mind.

I began to feel uncomfortably aware of how alone I was all day while Nick was at work. That familiar stir-crazy feeling I'd experienced in Bahrain descended, but this time it wasn't just the boredom that got under my skin. It was accompanied by a pang of loneliness. I'd spent far too much time rooting around in my own head while I was writing. After three days spent churning up the most emotionally draining parts of my life, reliving them step by step, and wrangling them onto the page, I needed a distraction from my thoughts and feelings. I needed human interaction.

I woke up on the sixth day feeling revitalised by the sensation of freedom. My self-isolation period was over. I was finally allowed to step foot outside the house and, on Nick's recommendation, I decided to get a taxi down the hillside to the beach club.

There was, of course, the obstacle of finding a taxi company. I poured over Google searches, trying to find a taxi company in the area and struggling to make sense of the Italian websites. I jotted down a few numbers that looked promising and then began formulating some backup notes in Italian using Google translate, just in case.

I rang the first number and nobody picked up. The second number was no longer in use. When I rang the third number, I was both relieved and a little nervous when I heard somebody pick up the phone and say, "Ciao."

"Ciao," I said and grabbed my notes. "Umm … Tu sai parlare inglese?"

"No," came the response. Perfect!

"Okay," I murmured, flipping to the next page of my notebook. "Posso avere un taxi … umm … da … err …"

"You WhatsApp?" the man asked, clearly losing patience with my incompetent Italian.

"Yes!"

"Send WhatsApp. I Google translate."

"Oh, that's great!" I said with relief. "Thank you." The line went dead.

I sent over my message, requesting a taxi from Nick's house to the beach club. I asked him to send it as soon as possible.

Taxi driver: *Not now. Too early.*

My heart sunk a little, wondering how long I'd have to wait.

Me: *What time?*

Taxi driver: *12*

I glanced at my watch. It was already 11:30.

Me: *Perfect!*

At 11:50, I gathered everything I needed into my bag, slathered myself with sunscreen, and headed outside to wait. Nick's house was nestled right in the corner of the little gated area. I made my way through the street and used the button to unlock the big metal gate at the entrance. I took a seat on the wall outside and waited.

Ten minutes went by, and a watched the cars rumble up and down the steep hill. A lady passed me on the other side of the road, walking her tiny fluff-ball of a dog.

"Ciao." I smiled over at her.

"Ciao," she replied, flashing her pretty smile.

Another 10 minutes slipped by and then another. I took off my huge straw hat and fanned myself with it quite aggressively. There was no shade I could retreat to, and it was getting unbearably hot. I sent the taxi operator another WhatsApp message, asking if someone was on their way. Then I waited some more.

Another 15 minutes passed, and the lady with the fluffy dog rounded the corner again, heading back home. She looked startled to see me, still sitting out in the midday sun, flushed pink and sweating profusely. She smiled at me with eyes that seemed to accuse me of being downright crazy and hurried past.

After over an hour of waiting, I gave up. The taxi operator had received and opened my message and hadn't responded. It was clear I was not going to make it to the beach that afternoon. I gathered up my things, hopped off the little wall, and turned back towards Nick's house.

When I opened the front door, cool, air-conditioned air spilled out to greet me. I went inside and stood directly under the air-conditioning unit for 10 minutes while I gulped down an entire litre of water. My whole body was pulsating with heat. The cold wafts of air from the ceiling felt incredible after sitting out in the sun for so long. Finally, my body began to cool down. I hopped into a cool shower and collapsed onto the bed.

That didn't exactly go according to plan.

I pulled out my laptop and started trying to formulate a new plan for tomorrow. I needed to get out and be around fellow humans. I needed a change of scenery. I trawled through Google again, this time looking for places I could visit within walking distance. There was nothing. With walking out of the question and taking a taxi clearly not the most reliable choice, I began looking for public transport that could get me to the beach. Or a pool. Or, quite frankly, anywhere with other human beings.

Midway down the long list of indecipherable websites, I saw a site for a nearby hotel that had its own shuttle service. I stopped. What if I booked myself into a hotel for a few nights? I could use the pool, explore somewhere new, and undoubtedly find people to talk to there. It would be like a mini-holiday within a holiday! Then, when Nick's streak of 12-hour shifts finished in a few days' time, I could come back and we could hang out together.

It was the perfect solution. It would be fun and exciting. I hesitated. Was I really about to flit off to a random hotel in Italy by myself? Suddenly, I felt terrified. I stopped. The loop of photos of the hotel continued to flash on my laptop screen.

What on earth am I afraid of?

I clicked the "Book" button.

Chapter 21

I woke up the next morning, tangled up in the blankets of the guest bed, and stared up at the ceiling. A thin strip of light was streaming in through a crevice in the shutters and glinted off the specks of dust that were suspended in the air.

I was nervous.

That same strange feeling of doubt was back. It was so heavy, it almost felt as though it were sitting right on my chest. I hoisted myself up onto my elbows and sat up in bed.

What's going on here?

I began to riffle through my thoughts, looking for an answer. A year before, I'd kept all my uncomfortable thoughts and feelings stuffed down in a locked box. I'd been terrified to go anywhere near them. But, by writing them down, I'd learned how to handle them properly. I could wade into the unpleasantness now to get to the bottom of those feelings and stop them from growing out of control. I'd got quite good at getting to the root of a problem when I took the time to rummage through my feelings.

Something about my sudden change of plans had triggered this unsettling sensation of doubt. It didn't seem to make any sense. I was going to a four-star hotel to lounge by the pool for a few days. Where was the problem?

It's not like I hadn't packed a bag and headed off on solo adventures before. I'd moved to Kuwait alone. I'd moved across the country to go to university alone. Heck, when I was in my early twenties, I'd spent four nights at a hostel in a sketchy part of New York City alone before catching the Greyhound to Boston. For the entire journey, I'd been stuck next to a man from Tennessee who was quite clearly unhinged and insisted on loudly regaling all of the other passengers with the story of how his best friend had stabbed him in the eye. If I could do all of that, why was I suddenly so uncomfortable with spending a couple of nights at a hotel at the bottom of the hill?

What if something goes wrong?

What could possibly go wrong? It's a 20-minute drive away. It's a nice hotel with good reviews …

I don't want to take any more risks!

Ah-ha!

It had been easy to feel safe and secure during lockdown … And all of the subsequent half-lockdowns and kind-of-sort-of-lockdowns that had followed. They had kept my world small and my opportunities limited. With limited opportunities came limited risk. Now that the world was opening up and letting real life flood back in, it felt like my sense of control was being washed away. I hadn't realised it until now, but I was scared. I was scared of making another wrong move and being knocked off my feet again. I was terrified of making any more mistakes. I let that sink in for a few minutes, watching the dust dance through the narrow shaft of sunlight in Nick's guestroom.

So what's the plan? Are you going to just hide under your bed for the rest of your life because you're afraid of messing up again?

I tossed the blankets to one side and slid out of bed. I picked up my case and began stuffing it with clothes for the next few days. There was no decision to be made. There was nothing to mull over. And there was absolutely no point in being afraid. I would mess up. I would undoubtedly continue to tumble through life making one mistake after another. By the time I reached 50, I'd probably have an entire stack of things I'd wish I'd done differently. That wasn't something to be afraid of and it certainly wasn't a reason to stop taking risks and snatching up adventures.

Agreeing to marry Dylan had been a mistake. We weren't right for each other. It was silly of me to have given up my entire life the way I had. But did I regret it? No, not anymore. If I hadn't done those things, I might never have had the cataclysmic eruption of emotions that forced me to heal from the past and learn to love myself. I wouldn't take that "mistake" back, so why should I spend a single second worrying about the mistakes I may or may not make in the future?

I zipped up my case and got dressed. Then I headed back down to the end of the road and through the metal gates where, to my relief, a black car was waiting for me.

My driver was a broad man with a round, friendly looking face. He must have been in his early thirties and was eager to make conversation with me when I discovered I spoke English.

"My English," he said, glancing at me in the rear-view mirror, "is not so good, but I like to practise."

"I think your English sounds very good," I assured him. Needless to say, it was infinitely better than my Italian.

He asked me about where I was from and what I did for a living, how long I'd been in Naples, and what I was doing there.

"I'm staying with a friend," I told him. "Just visiting."

He raised his eyebrows and smiled knowingly. "Your boyfriend?"

"No," I said, shaking my head for emphasis. "Just a friend."

"Where is your boyfriend?"

"I don't have a boyfriend." I laughed.

"No boyfriend?" He sounded genuinely shocked or perhaps concerned. "So you are alone."

"Yes." I pushed my sunglasses up the bridge of my nose and nodded. "I'm alone."

It was a short drive down to the hotel. It sat right at the base of the mountain I'd been overlooking all week from Nick's terrace. Smooth white walls ran around the outside and delicate trees veiled the property from the outside world. There was a steep, winding path that led up to the reception through a pretty green garden full of spindly trees and colourful flowers. The terracotta-coloured tiles led me right to the top of an incline and then back down some steps and into the cool shade of the reception.

"Ciao," said the man at the front desk as I walked in.

"Ciao. I have a room booked. I know check-in isn't for another hour, but is it okay if I sit by the pool and wait until the room is ready?"

"Of course!" he said with another smile. He took a copy of my passport and looked up my details on the computer system. "You will stay for two nights," he said, reading from the screen. "And you are alone."

"Yes, I'm alone," I said and wondered how many more times the Universe planned on clobbering me over the head with that fact today.

I left my suitcase in the reception area and headed down to the pool with my laptop. I followed the winding path back up the way I'd just come and then followed the signs that led me off to the right where a large pool area was tucked away behind a cluster of trees. I heard it before I saw it. The air rang with the sounds of laughter and splashing.

On one side of the pool stood a squat white building that looked like a restaurant. All of its large sliding doors had been pulled open, and tables and chairs spilled out onto the patio where small groups of people were gathered, playing card games and laughing loudly. On the other side of the pool was a gentle grass slope scattered with blue sunbeds. The entire area was packed with people and the warm air buzzed with the sounds of laughter and eager conversations.

Finally! Other people!

I waded through the haphazard rows of sunbeds and took a seat under a veranda. Then I opened up my laptop and began typing. The noisy world around me immediately melted away into the balmy haze of the background. I became so engrossed in writing that I didn't notice the sun climbing in the sky. It wasn't until I finished typing and let the world around me swim back into focus that I suddenly became very aware of how hot and sticky I was. It was midday, and everyone had taken shelter in what little relief the shade could offer from the heat. I rubbed my eyes and looked around.

The tables around me were full now. To my right, a large family of 12 or 13 people had squeezed around a long table. The smallest children struggled relentlessly to break free and scurry back to the pool while their parents did their best to entice them to eat their lunches. An elderly lady with a tiny frame sat and the head of the table, scowling at everyone and occasionally shouting a word or two in Italian. On the next table sat a young, bronzed couple with their chunky baby perched between them. They cooed at her softly in Italian and her entire face shone with an excited smile. To my left was a table full of older teens who were sprawled lazily over their chairs, picking at fries and chatting in Italian.

It hit me.

I glanced around the pool area, from one group of people to the next. I tried to discern individual voices amid the mingled sound of chatter. There was no denying it – I was the only person at that hotel who wasn't Italian. I suddenly felt uncomfortably aware of being the odd one out.

Nobody's going to notice.

I could not have been more wrong.

When it was time to check in, I heaved my unnecessarily heavy suitcase up the two flights of stairs to my room. I didn't stop to look around or take in the decor. Instead, I threw my case down on the floor, unzipped it hastily, and began digging around for my bikini. After sitting outside all morning in the heat of the summer, I was desperate to get in the pool.

When I got back down to the pool area, it was quieter than it had been when I first arrived. I managed to find myself a sunbed that was tucked away in a corner. I dragged it out from the shade and into the full blaze of the sun. Then I pulled out my copy of *Bleak House* and tried to get comfortable. I couldn't shake the feeling that people were looking at me, though. Every time I glanced up, I seemed to catch someone looking over in my direction. Was my blindingly pale skin really drawing that much attention?

"You are the English girl?" a voice said from above me. I snapped my head up and saw one of the restaurant's staff members standing next to my sunbed, looking down at me curiously.

"Well … British," I said with an awkward laugh.

"My English …" He made a gesture with his hand to indicate that it wasn't the best.

"Oh! My Italian is the same," I said, repeating the gesture. He smiled. Then his face suddenly became serious.

"You are in the sun," he said, struggling to find the words. "And you are too …" He gestured towards me with wide eyes. "White! Not like Italians," he added, pointing to his beautifully tanned skin. He wasn't wrong. I was practically translucent by comparison. "It's bad. The sun is bad for you."

"Well, I'm trying to be less white," I tried to explain. "I want to tan."

He stared at me in confusion. Perhaps it was because he didn't understand the words, or perhaps he thought that it was unthinkable that someone with skin so obviously prone to burning would choose to sit out in direct sunlight in the middle of the day.

"You sure?" he asked, still looking worried. I nodded. Before he left, he added, "You come … just you? Alone?" I nodded again and he raised his eyes in an expression that seemed to suggest that I was definitely insane.

As it turns out, everyone in the hotel thought I was odd. After all, there I was at an Italian hotel with barely a shred of Italian to string together, and I was there entirely alone. When I got up to get some water, I distinctly heard not one, but two people mutter the words "ragazza inglese" to their friends as I walked past. I tried to be inconspicuous and blend in with the crowd, but there was no getting away from the fact that my shockingly pale legs glowed like beacons.

It's really not that bad. It's mostly in your head.

"Miss …" I opened my eyes and saw the restaurant worker standing at the side of my sunbed again, looking worried. "Please go out from the sun."

Chapter 22

That evening, I sauntered down to the hotel restaurant for dinner. The air was thick with the hum of crickets. I followed the winding path down past the reception and along to the pool area. I was a little early, so I sat down next to the pool and opened up my copy of *Bleak House*.

I'd made my restaurant reservation on my way back from the pool, earlier on in the afternoon. I'd shuffled into the reception looking a little pink after an afternoon of sunbathing, and the friendly man at the desk had greeted me with a nod of recognition.

"Is everything okay?" he'd asked and I'd nodded.

"Yes, thank you. I just wondered if I could book a table at the restaurant for dinner tonight please?" I'd said.

"Just for one person?" he'd asked, looking a little surprised.

"Yes please." I had smiled and wondered for the hundredth time that day if I really was crazy for checking into a hotel alone.

"Just one second and I will check," he'd told me. He had picked up the phone from the desk and punched some numbers into the old-fashioned handset.

After a few rings, someone had answered and he'd begun an animated monologue in Italian. My ears had pricked up at the sound of the words "ragazza inglese" again, which was followed by a chuckle. "It's no problem," he'd assured me, putting the phone back down on the receiver.

"Thank you."

As I sat reading my book by the pool, more people started to arrive. They milled around the edge of the pool, waiting for the restaurant to open. I recognised a few faces from earlier on in the day. A few of them shot quizzical looks in my direction.

"Ragazza inglese …" I heard murmured from a few tables over.

It felt as though everyone was trying to figure out who this strange British girl was, traipsing around the hotel all alone.

Yeah, you and me both, guys.

Because that same heavy question still loomed over me – who the heck am I now? I'd made peace with where I'd been and I was taking steps every day to lead me to where I wanted to go. The only thing that still seemed a little hazy was who I was right now. For some reason, I still couldn't quite get that into focus.

A peel of laughter snapped me out of my trance. I looked around and saw that people had started filing into the restaurant, so I picked up my stuff and headed towards the door. As I approached the brusque-looking middle-aged man who was in charge of showing everyone to their tables, I opened my mouth to give my name but was cut off.

"English?" he said without hesitation.

Is it really that obvious it's me?

I nodded in surprise.

"Ah, okay!" He led me over to a table that was set for two. Another man quickly appeared from the other side of the restaurant to clear away the second place setting and to hand me a menu.

I felt entirely out of place. It wasn't just because, as the only non-Italian speaker there, I was entirely out of place. There was also the uncomfortable awkwardness of being alone. I'd never gone to dinner alone before and, sitting there at the centre of the restaurant at a table set for one, I felt exposed. I tucked a strand of hair behind my ear and picked up the menu in an attempt to look busy and purposeful. I scoured the page with furrowed brows. Of course, the whole thing was in Italian and, of course, I

237

couldn't decipher much of it. I was able to pick out the most basic Italian words and phrases and, after a few laboured minutes, I realised I was at a seafood restaurant. I took a nervous sip of water. I'm allergic to shellfish.

I pulled my phone out of my bag and sent a snapshot of the menu to my friend Amber with the caption, *"Is there anything on this menu I can eat without accidentally poisoning myself?"*

Amber and I were roommates at university. She's one of the most successful people I know, not to mention smart, sophisticated, and as resourceful as Liam Neeson in *Taken*. She also speaks three languages. There is no crisis that this woman can't handle.

After a few moments, she came back to me with an assurance that there was one pasta that was safe. She followed it up with a second message asking why on earth I would go to a seafood restaurant when I knew I was allergic to shellfish.

Me: *I booked myself into a hotel out in the middle of nowhere and everything is in Italian. I think everyone thinks I'm weird.*

Amber: *Yeah. Sounds like something you would do. I'll send you over some key phrases to get you through dinner.*

The waiter arrived at my table shortly afterwards and stared at me blankly, waiting for me to attempt to order. Using a combination of Amber's voice notes, the menu, and sheer determination, I ordered my dinner in shaky Italian, and the waiter gave me a brief nod before he left. I sat back and tried to relax. To my right, a huge, open window framed the view of the rugged mountainside. Houses were scattered here and there along the ledges, and the whole scene was set against the peachy pink of a sunset that was plastered across the sky. It was beautiful.

By the time the waiter brought my wine, the restaurant had started to fill up and the low hum of conversation had started to build to a cheerful babble. I recognised a few faces from earlier on in the day. The large, rambunctious family with the angry-looking grandmother was clustered around a long table near the entrance. On my other side, I noticed an older couple who had been muttering in my direction earlier on while I was sitting near the pool. The wife shot inquisitive glances at me over her bruschetta. On the table directly opposite me sat a young and glamorous-looking couple. I couldn't make out the man's face from where I was sitting, but the woman was gorgeous. Her thick, silky hair tumbled over her shoulders, and her huge, dark eyes fluttered up to the waiter as he approached their table.

She stopped him in his tracks to ask him something. Again, I heard the words "ragazza inglese", and glanced up in time to see her nod over in my direction with her eyebrows raised. The waiter nodded in reply and said something that all three surrounding tables laughed at and then headed back towards the kitchen.

Everyone is laughing at me because I'm alone.

Try to be optimistic – they may just be laughing at your terrible Italian.

I took another sip of wine and tried to brush off the discomfort. At that moment, the waiter brought out my pasta. I thanked him in the most convincing Italian I could and checked the bowl for any sign of shellfish before taking a bite. It was delicious. In fact, even if it had been laced with shrimp, it would have been worth a trip to A&E. I savoured every bite, trying my utmost not to just shovel the entire bowlful of pasta into my mouth in one go.

When the bowl was finally empty, I worked up the confidence (with the help of Amber's voice notes and more wine) to order a bowl of lemon-flavoured gelato. As the sunset splayed across the sky in different shades of deepening red through the frame of the open window, I ate my dessert and drank my wine, and let everything and everyone else around me fade into the background. I was in Italy. I was enjoying a delicious bowl of gelato and watching the sunset. I was alone, and admittedly that felt more than a little awkward, but the main thing was, I was enjoying myself. Just a few short months ago, I'd been unable to untangle myself from the folds of my duvet. I'd cried myself to sleep each night, wondering if it was possible that the unwavering throb of heartache would ever fade. Now that grey fog of hopelessness had lifted and I had stepped back out into the sunshine. That was all that mattered.

When the deep scarlet of twilight started to fade into night, I stopped the waiter as he passed my table.

"Mi scusi. Posso avere il conto per favore?" I asked with a newfound confidence that startled even me. He smiled and hurried off to get the bill.

"Molto bene!" the glamorous lady opposite me cried and clapped her hands. Her white teeth sparkled as she smiled at me, kindly. "It was so good." The members of the surrounding tables were smiling too. "You speak English?" she asked me.

"Yes," I said and smiled back at her.

"And you are here alone?" She raised her eyebrows again.

"Just me." I nodded, and this time I tried to inject a little more decisiveness into it.

She sat back in her seat and folded her arms, smiling even more. "Wow," she said. "But that's so amazing. Brave! It would like to do something the same, but …" She trailed off and shrugged, though I wasn't sure if it was because she couldn't find the words in English, or because she couldn't find the reasons that were holding her back. She turned to the table next to her where the inquisitive older lady was watching our conversation intently. She said something to her in Italian, and the older lady looked back in my direction with raised eyebrows again. Then she gave me a small smile.

The sounds of the restaurant followed me as I walked along the pathway that led back to my room. Above me, the brightest stars were already fighting to glow against a sky still streaked with the last remnants of sunlight.

I collapsed onto my bed and sighed. I was in Italy alone. Suddenly, that didn't seem awkward or uncomfortable. It was incredible! Last summer, I was so embarrassed by the state of my own life that I'd cowered down behind a shelf of bread in the corner shop. Somehow, between then and now, I'd mustered the courage to book myself this trip, take myself to dinner all by myself, and attempt to string together enough Italian to order my meal. Had I ever taken so much as a second to appreciate how far I'd really come? The beautiful lady in the restaurant was right – I was brave. I might not always feel like it, but that's exactly what I was. All this time, I'd been scratching around, trying to find a new way to define myself based on the way my life looked. None of that mattered. I knew who I was now. I was a freaking badass!

I meandered down to the pool the next morning, sat down at a table, and pulled my laptop out of my bag. The sun hadn't rounded the tips of the mountains yet, so the entire area was still dipped in a cool shade. I got comfortable in my seat and began tapping away at the keys again. I didn't need to pause to think about the words. They simply dived straight out of my brain and flashed up on the laptop screen in front of my eyes.

I sat there, typing up the story of the most painful days of my life, for over an hour. Then I sat back in the chair and stared at the screen in silence. The cursor blinked at me expectantly. Part two of my book was finished. I had traced my heartbreak from the moment of its conception right through to my turning point for the better. I'd given words to all of the emotions that had been caged up inside my head. I'd let all of the fears and obsessions, toxic thoughts, and melancholy musings out from the confines of my mind and set them free.

Something about telling my own story – revisiting it and reliving it – had taken the sting out of it. By working through the whole ordeal from start to finish, I'd made sense of it. It wasn't just a crushing jumble of emotion anymore. It was a linear series of events and, as sad as they had been to experience, they were finally in the past. And I could finally appreciate everything they had taught me.

The sun was beginning to creep around the mountaintops, and the first bright rays were stretching out across the grass. I felt different; I felt lighter. I felt more like myself than I had in a long time. I saved the file on my laptop and headed back up to my room to get dressed for a day of lazing by the pool.

I got dressed and picked up my bag. As I was heading back out the door, I caught a glimpse of myself in the mirror and stopped. I still didn't recognise her; she had changed so much in the last year. She'd gone from a starry-eyed bride-to-be to a torn-down shadow of herself with black-rimmed eyes and a gaunt face. Now she'd changed again. Faint worry lines had etched themselves into her skin, and her face was rounder now than it had been before. She stood tall. She was confident. I didn't recognise her because I'd never seen this version of her before. But I liked it.

I went down to the pool and settled onto one of the sunbeds that I'd lined up with the sun. I soaked up the warmth from the growing sunshine and let the soothing sound of the indecipherable conversations all around me blend into a beautiful hum. I was completely and utterly relaxed.

I spent the remnants of the morning, and the first few hours of the afternoon enjoying this newfound tranquility. I dozed in and out of consciousness in the warmth of the morning sunshine. Then, when the heat got to be too much, I waded into the pool and let the glistening water cool me down. I did a few lazy laps, and stopped so I could look through the restaurant and out onto the same mountain view I had marvelled at the night before. I rested my head in my crossed arms and sighed.

"Miss," came a voice from above me. I looked up, squinting into the sunlight, and saw the man who had been so concerned about my unusually pale skin in the sun yesterday.

"Ciao," I said, smiling up at him.

"This," he said proudly, producing a tub from the table behind him and handing it down to me. "A gift from me." I took the tub of lemon sorbet gratefully and thanked him. "Because," he said slowly in his thick accent, "is hot." He gestured up at the sun and then shrugged down at me. "And you …"

"Are so white," I joined in with a smile. "Thank you! Grazie!"

I ate my sorbet, still semi-submerged in the pool and gazing up at the rugged view of the mountains in the distance. I don't think there was anything particularly transformative about that moment. Granted, I was enjoying a delicious lemon sorbet on a gloriously sunny day and soaking in the stunning views of Naples. I'm sure all of those things did wonders to lift my mood. There was no reason why, however, in that particular moment of all the moments I'd had, I should suddenly notice that the answer to that looming question had been right there all along.

My name is Aimée. It doesn't matter where I am, what I do for work or what my relationship status is. None of those things defines me. I'm me! And I am enough, just as I am.

Afterword

And she lived happily …

That wasn't the end. It wasn't the end of my story (because – spoiler alert – I'm still living my life!), and it wasn't the end of me working on myself. This isn't another cheesy chick-flick and my problems didn't all magically melt away in the Italian sun as I ate my lemon sorbet. In fact, there were plenty more low points after I got back from Italy. There were tears and moments of self-doubt, and I can guarantee that there will be plenty more tears and moments of self-doubt in the future.

I've learned to remind myself every day that I am enough. That doesn't mean that I always believe it. Some days everything I've learned about loving myself flies up in the air and I start to doubt myself. I can't begin to tell you how many times I've doubted myself while writing this book. There were days when I thought the imposter syndrome would eat me from the inside out!

The thing is, the road to becoming a happier, more fulfilled and content version of yourself isn't a straight line from start to finish. It's like a game of snakes and ladders. One minute, you're moving along quite nicely, minding your own business, and feeling like a total badass. The next, you find yourself winding back down the board where you get spat out in the same place you were a few months ago. It's frustrating, but you've got to keep moving forwards.

A lot of people ask me how long it took to get over the breakup with Dylan. I'd love to tell you, but it's an impossible question to answer. Some days, I would wake up feeling like I was completely over it, only to wake up a few days later feeling sick with the absence of him all over again. I think the hurt wore away so slowly that I barely even noticed it. I can tell you this, though – it took a long time!

Now I honestly say I'm glad that everything happened the way that it did. It was a difficult thing to go through, but it brought me to where I am right now. I am content and Sophie was right – contentment is better than happiness. Happiness comes and goes with things outside of yourself. A cookie can make you happy. Stepping in a puddle with your new boots on can snatch that happiness away. Contentment comes from within, and it's powerful!

Contentment comes from knowing you're enough, just as you are. And you are! You're deserving of love, happiness, and respect, right now in this very moment. You don't need to earn that "enough-ness". You don't have to wait until you lose five pounds or get a new job or have more Instagram followers. The wonderful thing is, once you realise you're enough and you don't need any of those external things to feel truly content and fulfilled, nobody can ever take that away from you. It's yours to keep! I no longer worry about getting my heart broken, because I know that a man has the potential to add to my foundation of contentment, but he can never take away from it. It's mine. It comes 100% from me.

I also know that with this newfound respect for myself, I'll never let anyone convince me that I'm not enough again. And neither should you.

So the story doesn't really end here. This isn't my happily-ever-after. This is just the start.

About the Author

Aimée Rebecca is no stranger to misadventures and plot-twists.   She was born and raised in Wales and spent several years living in Kuwait and then Bahrain during her twenties. Aimée has built a substantial following on social media, where she shares her unique brand of unfiltered, down-to-earth positivity. In 2021 she created *The This Time Next Year Challenge*, which has reached tens of thousands of people and encouraged them to make meaningful, sustainable change in their lives. *Just As I Am* is Aimée's debut publication…and was heavily fuelled by coffee.

▶ Aimee Rebecca
📷 @aimee_oddball
♪ @aimee_oddball

Printed in Great Britain
by Amazon